This book belongs to

_____

_____

_____

ALEX AND PENNY IN EGYPT
THE MYSTERY OF THE 9 SCARABS

THE MAIN CHARACTERS OF THIS STORY ARE:

ALEX AND PENNY

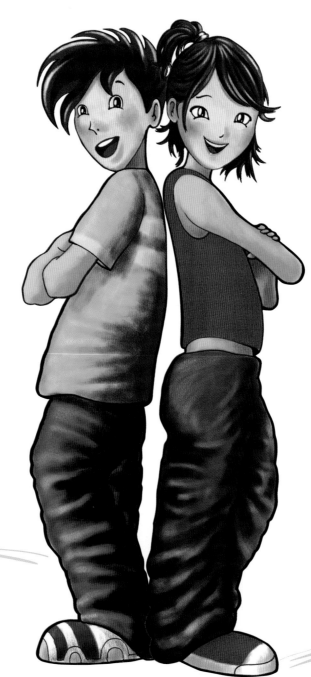

I'm Alex, Penny's brother. They say I'm a computer whiz.... Actually, without meaning to boast, I'm much more than that: an Internet genius, a videogame wizard and the world gaming champion!
Unlike that know-it-all sister of mine, they say that I'm always in trouble and that if I can't find any, I invent some. It's just that I'm adventurous, really!

What about you?
Write to my e-mail address to tell me all about yourself:

alex@whitestar.it

Hi! I'm Penny, Alex's sister. We're twins, but we don't resemble each other at all. To start with, I'm older than him… by five minutes! I love drawing and want to be a famous painter when I grow up. Alex calls me "Miss Know-It-All" and says that I'm the smart aleck of the family, but the truth is that I adore reading books, stories and comics. However, there are plenty of things that I don't know – for example, I'm hopeless at math!

What do you like?
Write to my e-mail address to tell me all about yourself:

penny@whitestar.it

Epsilon and its inventor, Kappa

WS SPECIAL AGENTS!

It all started when we read a very strange announcement in the newspaper: "Seeking agents willing to deal with risks and danger; great smartness and cunning required." How could we resist the temptation? When we answered we met Kappa, who's a brilliant inventor (though absolutely hopeless at disguises).... Kappa explained that in order to take part in the adventures promised in the announcement, we'd have to prove our courage and smartness by trying to discover what was hidden behind the mysterious WS agency! We thus set off for an adventure in the skies above Italy, aboard Epsilon, a super-technological hot-air balloon, discovering curious facts about the country's most famous monuments. We followed the clues to the WS headquarters, where we met Cornelius Misterius, the general director of the World Secret Investigation Agency, which investigates unsolved mysteries all over the world. And that's how we became special agents! Who knows what our next adventure will be?

Cornelius Misterius

"Darn it, Alex! Stop going on about mummies! If you'd been quiet for a moment and listened to the guide, then you'd know that the mummies are displayed in the last room. We're going to see the jewelry now."

"Jewelry? Bah! That's girl's stuff! I want to see the –"

"That's enough, Alex!"

Alex sighed and sunk into an offended silence, to Penny's great relief. His sister just didn't understand: visiting a museum was a wonderful new thing for him! He'd always thought that it was very boring wandering around inside among broken vases, silently listening to the words of a guide, but Alex hadn't hesitated a moment when Penny had asked him to visit the exhibition on the pharaohs with her. Ever since they'd torn through the Egyptian Museum in Turin looking for clues to the location of the WS headquarters, the twins had been fascinated by the mysterious ancient civilization, and even Alex had tried to find out more, in his own way. As Penny leafed through dusty art books in an even dustier library, her brother surfed the Web seeking information on Egypt, and fuelling his deep fascination with mummies. He couldn't wait to see a real one, as his sister made him listen to the umpteenth description of a priceless necklace. Alex started to look around in boredom and suddenly caught a glimpse of something moving among the crowd… NO! It couldn't be! He'd seen…

"Penny! Penny! A mummy!"

"Alex, I'm fed up with you! I'm not joking, you know. Did you hear me? If you don't stop talking about mummies, I'll…"

But Alex didn't hear his sister's threat, for he suddenly seemed to be turned to stone, like one of the granite statues of the pharaohs.

"Alex? Now you've got me worried, what's wrong?" asked Penny, and followed Alex's pointing finger with her gaze to see a mummy!

A real mummy, with bandages and all, that was trying to hide behind a statue.

"OK, Alex, we've got to work out what's going on. You were dying to see a mummy, right? Well, let's go and take a look!"

"Penny, you must be crazy! It could be dangerous! And what if we lose the guide?" But Penny was already walking towards the statue and there was nothing that Alex could do except sigh and follow her reluctantly. When they were just a couple of steps from the statue, Alex saw a few inches of bandage sticking out from behind the plinth. Determined not to let himself be surprised by an old mummy, he grabbed the bandage and started tugging it hard towards him.

"Stop! Stop, Alex, you're ruining my disguise!"

"KAPPA!" exclaimed the twins in amazement.

The gold mask of the pharaoh Tutankhamen

Egypt is situated in the northeast corner of Africa. The Sahara Desert covers most of its land area, but it is also crossed by the Nile River, which creates a fertile narrow valley that is fit for habitation.

Egypt

USEFUL FACTS

CAPITAL: Cairo (the location of the largest Egyptian museum in the world)

LANGUAGE: Arabic

CLIMATE: HOT! During the day the temperature can rise above 120 degrees F.

Here I am with my camel Jamal! The Bedouin (desert nomad) who lent me Jamal told me that camels can go without drinking for days. Indeed, these animals are able to survive on the water that they drink before setting out into the desert and on the fat stored in their humps.

"What are you doing here, Kappa?" Alex asked, disappointed that there was not a real mummy roaming around the museum.

"And, most importantly, why are you wrapped in bandages?" added Penny, trying not to laugh.

"It's my disguise, of course! Do you think I've overdone it? And what do you mean 'what are you doing here?' Have you forgotten that you're WSI agents? I'm here because I've got a mission for you!"

"A MISSION! What sort of mission? Tell us, Kappa!"

"Oh no, Misterius will tell you about it. Now I'll put you through to him on the miniature computer that I've invented…. Where did I put it? Here it is, between the bandages on my knee! Ah no, it's behind my elbow… um, perhaps I need to fine-tune it a little, but here it is anyway."

The twins saw the smiling face of Misterius, the general director of the World Secret Investigation Agency, appear on the tiny screen.

"Hello kids! Are you ready for a new adventure? We're sending you to Egypt."

"YEAH!" replied the children enthusiastically.

"Perfect! Here's the mystery that you must solve. A secret tunnel leading into the Sphinx has been discovered."

"Into the Sphinx? Do we have to go inside the Sphinx?"

"Yes, Alex, go inside and find out where the tunnel leads. I know that you already know a lot about Egypt, but I've prepared a guidebook to help you; I think it will come in very handy. It contains lots of information on the various aspects of the country and the ancient Egyptian civilization, plus all the personal notes that I've put together during my previous journeys. Secret Agent Kappa, give the kids my guide, please."

"Certainly, boss!"

"Contact me when you're in Egypt and have a good trip!" ended Misterius, waving. When his picture had disappeared from the little screen, Kappa gave Penny Misterius' guide, which was packed with loose papers and photographs. Then the inventor turned towards Alex and whispered, "I've got a surprise for you too, or rather, two surprises: the first is Epsilon's new engine. Just wait until you see how fast the hot air balloon travels now! The second is this 'micro-translator' device," he explained, showing Alex what looked like a colored button. "When it's worn by someone speaking a foreign language, it will immediately translate everything he or she says."

"Wow! Thanks, Kappa!"

"And now you'd better be on your way, because it's already late!"

Here's the Sphinx seen from the hot air balloon. Don't you think it looks like a real lion?

DID YOU KNOW?

One day Prince Thutmose IV stopped to rest in the shadow of the Sphinx, which was almost entirely buried by the desert sands. The statue appeared to him in a dream, and said, "Free me from this sand and I promise that you will become pharaoh in return." The young man did not forget the dream and ordered the statue to be restored. After having become pharaoh, as promised, Thutmose IV placed the "Dream Stele," a stone bearing this story, between the paws of the Sphinx.

Kappa had made some incredible changes to Epsilon's supersonic engines, allowing the hot air balloon to travel faster than ever!

Alex checked Epsilon's computer map. There was no doubt about it: they were in Egypt.

"Hold on tight, Penny, we'll be landing soon. It seems impossible, but we're here already, and unless the computer's wrong, we should be able to see..."

"The Pyramids! The Sphinx!" yelled Penny, leaning over the edge of the basket.

"That's where we need to land, behind the Sphinx, where Misterius says the entrance to the tunnel is located. The Sphinx certainly is impressive! It looks like a real lion, guarding the Pyramids... what's the matter?" added Alex, noticing that Penny was staring at him in amazement.

"You astound me sometimes with your intuition, even though you know nothing about history or art," Penny answered.

"Is that supposed to be a compliment? What sort of intuition are you talking about?"

"The Sphinx really does have a lion's body, while its face is believed to be a portrait of the pharaoh Chephren. The statue was built around 4500 years ago and is 240 feet long, 20 feet wide and 65 feet tall."

"Darn! How come you always know everything?" asked Alex, exasperated.

"Actually, I was reading the guidebook that Misterius compiled for us. You should take a look. It would do you good to read a bit."

"What use would that be? I've got you, my little encyclopedia."

"Very funny, Alex, but if you think that –" Penny suddenly broke off, looking ahead: the balloon had landed and now the twins were right in front of the entrance to the tunnel that they had come to explore. The opening was very narrow and also seemed very dark in the blinding desert sunlight. Their eyes got used to the dimness after a few steps inside, though, and the twins realized that they were in a passageway with a strong white light at the other end.

"Alex, what's that light? Where's it coming from?"

"There's only one way to find out, Penny. Let's go see!"

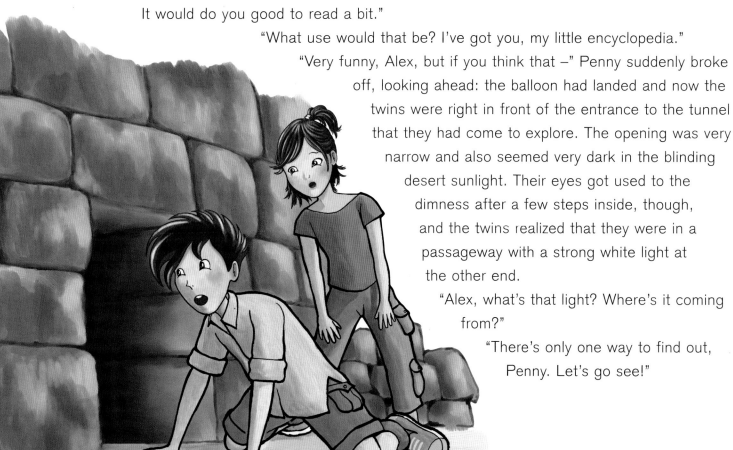

"Ooooh!" exclaimed the twins in amazement, as a real-life boy with a cat suddenly emerged from the bright light that was now slowly fading.

"Who are you? Where did you come from?" The astounded twins asked the boy, who was looking around in surprise. But their astonishment grew when the boy started to speak: " 𓀀𓏏𓆣 𓇋𓆓 𓊃𓏤 𓈖𓏏 𓂀𓏭 𓅓𓏏𓀀 "

"Wow! What language do you speak? Just a moment: I know!" Alex slowly approached the boy and fastened Kappa's universal translator to his tunic. "This should do the trick. We should be able understand each other now. What's your name?"

"I'm Nefer, and this is my cat, Mew. This morning Mew ran away and darted into the Sphinx and I followed her back, but we both fell into that vortex of light. Who are you? Your clothes are so strange!"

"I'm Penny, and this is my brother Alex. Where are you from, Nefer?"

"I'm from Thebes, but this morning I went with my father to inspect the pyramids, because the pharaoh will visit soon, and everything has to be perfect!"

"The pharaoh? Thebes? Your clothes…" Penny suddenly understood. "Nefer," she exclaimed in a weak voice, "you're from ancient Egypt!"

"Of course, Penny! You're a genius! And that vortex of light was a sort of time portal! Like in that science-fiction story I read –"

"WHAT! Do you mean I'm… in the future?" asked Nefer, his voice shaking.

"I'm afraid so, pal."

"AAAAARGH! I WANT TO GO HOME!!" cried Nefer, and burst into tears.

"Nef, don't cry! We'll help you return home," promised Alex, trying to calm him.

"SNIFF! And how will you manage that?" sobbed Nefer.

"Hmmm, let's see… How will we manage that, Penny? Are you listening to me? This is a very serious situation! Do you really think this is the right time to be admiring hieroglyphics? You don't even understand them!"

"I don't, but perhaps Nefer does. Can you try reading this inscription? It's right above the stone door through which you came and I think it could be important."

"All right, – sniff – this is more or less what it says: 'I, high priest of the mighty Ra,' blah, blah, blah… 'have discovered a doorway allowing access to distant worlds. Its power is infinite and it must never fall into the wrong hands. I have created a magic key to protect it.'"

"Perfect!" Alex exclaimed. "We'll find the key and reopen the door!"

"Listen, there's more: 'The key has been divided into nine identical pieces, each of which has the form of a sacred scarab.'"

"OK, let's look for nine scarab-keys then!"

"Wait a moment, it also says: 'Each scarab has been entrusted to one of my most faithful priests to be hidden in a sacred site in Egypt.'"

"Great, that's very clear: we have to find nine scarab-keys, each hidden in a different sacred place in Egypt, without knowing where to start…. We'll never be able to do it!" cried Alex, shaking his head.

"Who says we don't know where to start?" asked Penny, pointing to a low relief near the door. "What does that remind you of?" The picture reminded Alex of a long-stemmed flower with a triangular bloom, surrounded by cockroaches, as far as he could make out…

"It's a flower, and it needs spraying, with all those bugs around it."

"They're scarabs, not bugs, Alex! Nine scarabs… doesn't that ring any bells? I'll help you. That's not a flower, just compare it with the map of Egypt in Misterius' guidebook: it's the Nile! The stem is the river and the triangular bloom is its great delta! This is a map showing the hiding places of the nine scarabs! There are no place names, but look at the first one… it's very close to where we landed… and what's near the Sphinx?"

"The Pyramids!" exclaimed Alex and Nefer together.

"Let's go then, we must enter the Pyramids and find the first scarab."

And with that, Penny walked towards the exit, determined.

"Is your sister always such a genius, Alex?"

"She sure is… and you can't imagine how annoying it is having a genius in the family!"

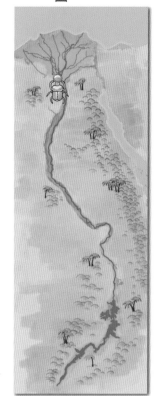

Alex was the first to emerge from the tunnel. He got up, shook the sand from his clothes, and let his eyes roam over the sight that opened up before him: the Giza Plateau and the three imposing Pyramids. These monuments are considered one of the symbols of Egypt and Alex, like everyone, had seen them hundreds of times on television, in his schoolbooks and on the Web, but no picture had ever conveyed the sensation that he was experiencing now. He felt incredibly small faced with the majestic panorama. He turned towards Penny, who was clambering out of the tunnel, and asked, "Have you ever seen such a magnificent sight?"

"Wow! It's simply –"

"A TERRIFYING SIGHT!! IT'S HORRIBLE!"

The twins ran towards Nefer, who had just emerged from the tunnel and was surveying his surroundings, eyes open wide, trembling and clasping Mew tightly in his arms. The twins exchanged a worried glance. "Nefer, calm down and remember to breathe!" The little Egyptian seemed terrified and continued to stare at the pyramids and tourist buses traveling over the plateau. "What… what are those… those things? And the pyramids… are all damaged…

and the Sphinx," Nefer raised his head to look at the great Sphinx. His eyes widened he and pointed, remarking in a wavering voice, "Its nose is missing!" And with that, he promptly fainted.

"NEFER!" The twins helped revive him, fanning him with a handkerchief and sprinkling him with water from their flask. As Nefer opened his eyes, Penny realized what had happened to him and gently explained, "Nef, today has been very tiring for you because you've traveled 3000 years through time, which certainly can't have been easy."

"Of course you feel a bit confused," added Alex understandingly.

"Right," Penny continued, "Right now, you're seeing Egypt as it is today. You'll probably see lots of things that have changed during our journey, as many centuries have passed. We'll help you to return home to your own time, where everything will be exactly as you left it this morning. You must be strong and stay calm."

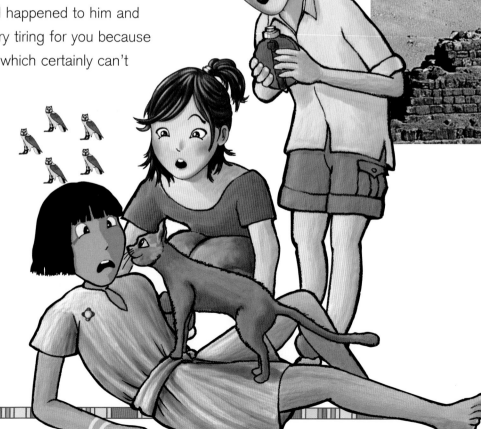

Mycerinus

Cheops

Chephren

The three Pyramids of the Giza Plateau were built by three pharaohs of the Old Kingdom: Cheops, Chephren and Mycerinus, around 4500 years ago!

"That's right. After all, you're our guide to the mysteries of ancient Egypt," added Alex, "and you're the only one who can help us take you home." Nefer didn't speak for a moment. Then he slowly rose, put Mew down, and shook the sand from his clothes. When he looked up again the twins were relieved to see that he was smiling. "You're right! I want to go home and I'll help you as much as I can, telling you everything I know!"

"Great, Nefer!" yelled the twins together.

"Let's start with the Pyramids," added Penny. "What can you tell us about the Pyramids?"

DID YOU KNOW?
The labor of over 30,000 men was required to build the Pyramids. The laborers were mostly peasants who worked on the construction site during the season during which the Nile flooded and the fields could not be cultivated.

WHAT ARE THE PYRAMIDS?

The Pyramids are the funerary monuments that the pharaohs of the Old Kingdom built to guard their tombs. We do not know why they chose such an unusual shape, although it is certain that the pyramid had a deep symbolic meaning for the Egyptians: it represented the hill from which the world was believed to have originated and recalled the rays of the sun, which were the symbol of Ra, the most important deity of the Egyptian religion. The size of the monuments celebrated the pharaoh's power, and consequently each new ruler tried to build a pyramid more imposing than that of his predecessor. Over 80 pyramids were built along the banks of the Nile between 2700 and 1640 BC, and the largest and best-preserved of these are the three famous Pyramids of Giza.

Step pyramid

The pyramid houses a maze of tunnels and secret passages!

WHO "INVENTED" THE PYRAMID?

DO YOU WANT TO KNOW THE NAME OF THE BRILLIANT EGYPTIAN ARCHITECT? WRITE THE ANSWERS TO THE CLUES IN THE STEPPED PYRAMID, AND YOU'LL BE ABLE TO READ HIS NAME IN THE HIGHLIGHTED SQUARES AT THE END.

1- The ninth letter of the alphabet
2- The beginning of mastaba
3- The first half of the pharaoh of the Great Pyramid
4- The precious material of Tutankhamen's mask
5- The Pyramids protected those of the pharaohs
6- Chephren, Mycerinus and... the pharaoh of the Great Pyramid

The oldest tombs were called *mastabas*, an Arabic word meaning "bench." And they were rectangular, just like a bench, and not at all like the Pyramids! However, a great change occurred during the reign of King Djoser, whose brilliant court architect decided to build a second, smaller mastaba on top of the first one. He was not satisfied with the result, though, for he wanted a far more imposing monument! So he built a third mastaba on top of the second, followed by a fourth, a fifth and finally a sixth. Placing six mastabas on top of each other enabled him built a monument resembling a stairway, which was 200 feet high. This was the first "stepped pyramid" from which all others originated, even those with perfectly smooth sides, like the Great Pyramid of Cheops.

THE GREAT PYRAMID...

...really does deserve its name: it was 482 feet tall and each side measured 755 feet! The pyramid is made from more than 2 million blocks of limestone, each of which weighs over 2 tons. You can imagine how difficult it must have been to transport them.

HOW TO BUILD A PYRAMID:

6 ESSENTIAL TIPS FOR YOUNG PHARAOHS

1 - Choose the site for your pyramid carefully: it must be perfectly level (it is not dignified for a pharaoh to have a crooked pyramid) and close to a limestone quarry, so that the workers can transport the huge blocks more easily (don't forget that the blocks are dragged to the pyramids using sleds, ramps and rollers).

2 - The architects can now draw the outline of the pyramid in the sand, taking care to orient the sides towards the four cardinal points: north, south, east and west.

3 - Let the building commence! The limestone blocks are brought from the quarries and laid to form the first level.

4 - The base of the pyramid is now ready. The workers must erect ramps to allow the huge limestone blocks to be transported above the first level and construct the subsequent stories, which gradually decrease in size with height, until completing the pyramid with the pointed tip.

5 - Remember that a maze of tunnels and secret passages must be built inside your pyramid to protect your burial chamber.

6 - Once finished, your pyramid won't look very elegant. We advise you, oh generous future pharaohs, to face the rough surface with white limestone blocks smoothed with chisels and to cover the tip with a gleaming precious material, such as gold, to give your pyramid a more sophisticated look in keeping with the latest fashions!

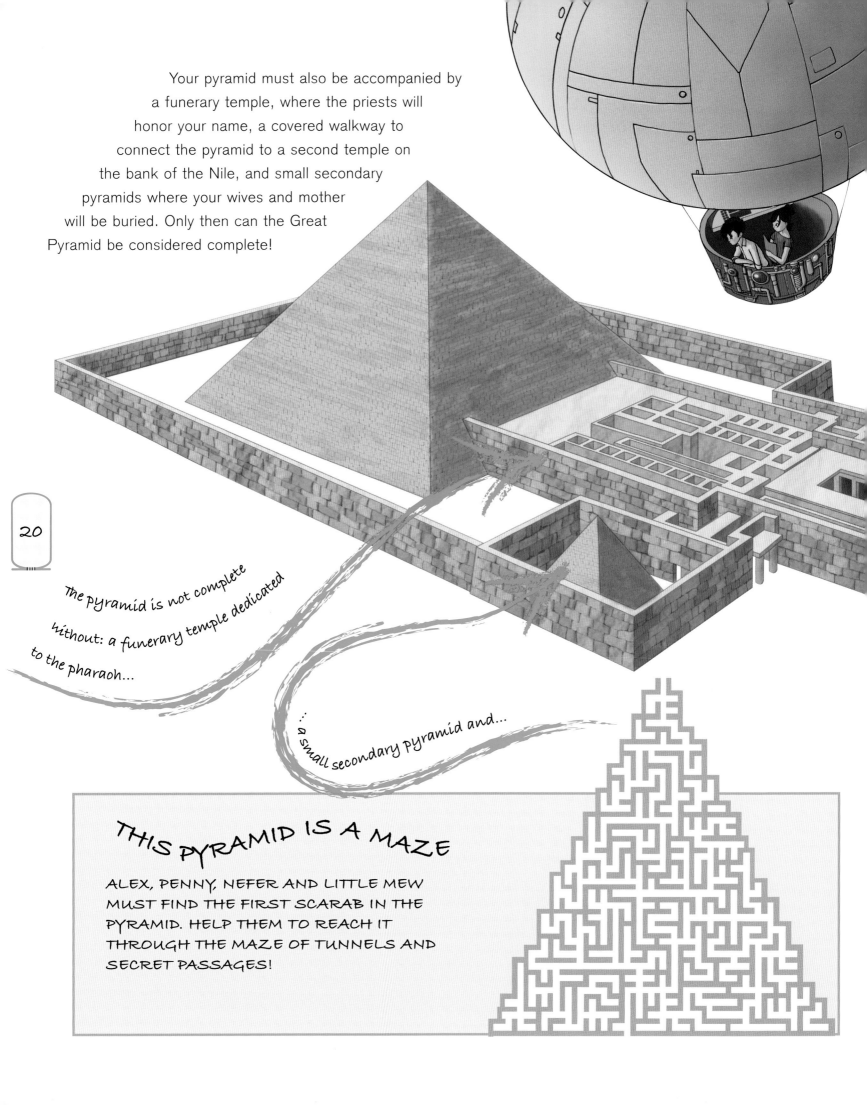

Your pyramid must also be accompanied by a funerary temple, where the priests will honor your name, a covered walkway to connect the pyramid to a second temple on the bank of the Nile, and small secondary pyramids where your wives and mother will be buried. Only then can the Great Pyramid be considered complete!

The pyramid is not complete without: a funerary temple dedicated to the pharaoh...

...a small secondary pyramid and...

THIS PYRAMID IS A MAZE

ALEX, PENNY, NEFER AND LITTLE MEW MUST FIND THE FIRST SCARAB IN THE PYRAMID. HELP THEM TO REACH IT THROUGH THE MAZE OF TUNNELS AND SECRET PASSAGES!

WHICH IS THE RIGHT DOOR?

THE CHILDREN HAVE MANAGED TO REACH THE END OF THE MAZE OF TUNNELS, BUT ARE NOW FACED WITH SIX DOORS. WHICH ONE HIDES THE SCARAB? IN ORDER TO FIND OUT, WRITE 3 NUMBERS ON EACH SIDE OF THE PYRAMID SO THAT THE SUM OF EACH SIDE IS ALWAYS 20. THE NUMBER AT THE TOP OF THE PYRAMID WILL SHOW THE CHILDREN WHICH DOOR TO OPEN.

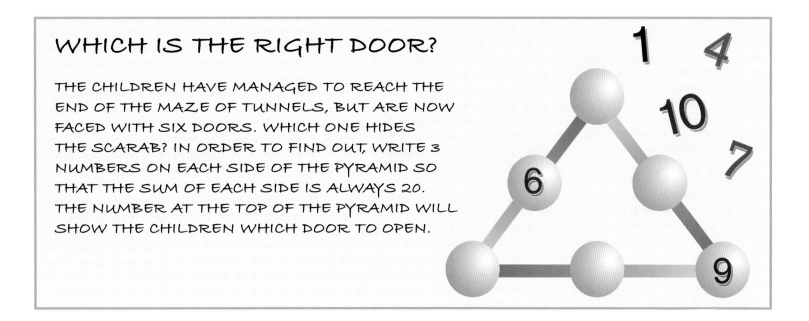

1 4 10 7 6 9

"Here it is at last!"

Alex picked up the scarab and showed it to Nefer so that he could decipher the inscription on it.

"What does it say, Nef?" asked the twins.

"Listen to this: 'In order to discover your next destination, you must prove your shrewdness by solving the puzzle engraved on the scarab.' Do you understand? Each time we must solve the puzzle of the scarab in order to find out where to go next!"

...a covered processional ramp.

THE PUZZLE OF THE SCARAB

FIND AND CROSS OUT THE FOLLOWING WORDS IN THE GRID, READING VERTICALLY OR HORIZONTALLY. THE REMAINING LETTERS WILL FORM THE NAME OF THE NEXT DESTINATION.

....

C	H	E	O	P	S	P
D	O	K	G	A	P	Y
J	A	Z	I	G	H	R
O	R	W	R	N	I	A
S	A	E	L	I	N	M
E	H	S	A	K	X	I
R	P	T	O	M	B	D

PHARAOH
CHEOPS
DJOSER
NILE
SPHINX
PYRAMID
GIZA
WEST
TOMB
GO

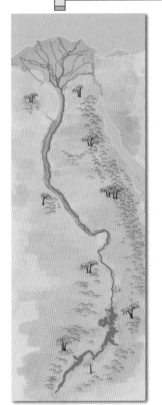

"This is Epsilon," said Alex, proudly pointing to the yellow hot air balloon, which had previously been hidden behind one of the Sphinx's paws.

"You came here in that? What is it exactly?" asked Nefer, perplexedly.

"It's MY hot air balloon," answered Alex, quickly correcting himself after catching a sharp glance from Penny, "I mean OUR hot air balloon. Right, Penny?" he added, smiling apologetically.

"Yes, it's ours, Alex! And to answer your question, Nef, we came here in Epsilon, which is very handy and very fast! It lets you fly up to…"

"Fly? Are you saying that this thing flies?"

"Of course! This little gem flies and is incredibly fast!" answered Alex indignantly. "Climb in and I'll show you what it can do."

Shaking his head in disbelief, Nefer clambered into what looked to him like a kind of enormous chariot without horse or wheels, followed by Mew. Alex took the controls, fired up Epsilon and allowed the balloon to take off without a bump – so gently that Nefer didn't even notice. "Flying, huh!" the little Egyptian muttered to himself. "What we need to do is find a boat sailing up the Nile to Thebes and ask for a ride! The Nile is the fastest way to travel in Egypt. Flying! You know, I almost fell for that, Alex! But everyone knows that people can't fly!"

The Nile is the world's longest river. It empties into the Mediterranean after a journey of over 4150 miles!

"Well, a few things have changed in 4000 years," answered Alex, grinning.

"Nef, please lean out a little and see if we're headed in the right direction," added Penny, with the same amused expression as her brother.

"Of course. I'm your guide and I'll show you the way. Just let me have a look and… AAAARRGGHHH! We're flying! We're flying! Come take a look! It's fantastic! Down there! That's old Father Nile!"

Alex and Penny burst out laughing at the sight of Nefer leaping enthusiastically from side to side and leaning dangerously out of the basket to see the land unfolding below. However, Mew reacted very differently to the new experience, jumping down from the edge of the basket and seeking refuge in Penny's arms. Penny held the trembling animal tightly and started to stroke her. After having calmed the cat, Penny remembered a strange expression that Nefer had used to indicate the river below. "Nef, you called the Nile 'old Father' and said that it's the fastest way to travel. What did you mean? Why is the Nile so important for Egypt?"

"For thousands of reasons!"

"Well, we've got plenty of time before we get to Karnak," said Alex, after having consulted the onboard computer. "Tell us about it, Nef."

DID YOU KNOW?

Every year, the Nile overflowed its banks and completely flooded the surrounding countryside. Instead of despairing, the peasants celebrated the event because they knew that once the water had dried, the fields would be covered with a layer of silt, which made the soil incredibly fertile. This dark silt was so important for the Egyptians that they called their country the Black Land.

DO YOU WANT TO KNOW HOW TO SAY "BLACK LAND" IN EGYPTIAN? DISCOVER ONE OF EGYPT'S NAMES BY COLORING THE SPACES MARKED WITH A DOT. THE LETTERS WILL APPEAR AS IF THEY ARE COVERED IN SILT.

A DAY ON THE BANKS OF THE NILE

The life of the peasants on the fertile banks of the Nile was very busy.

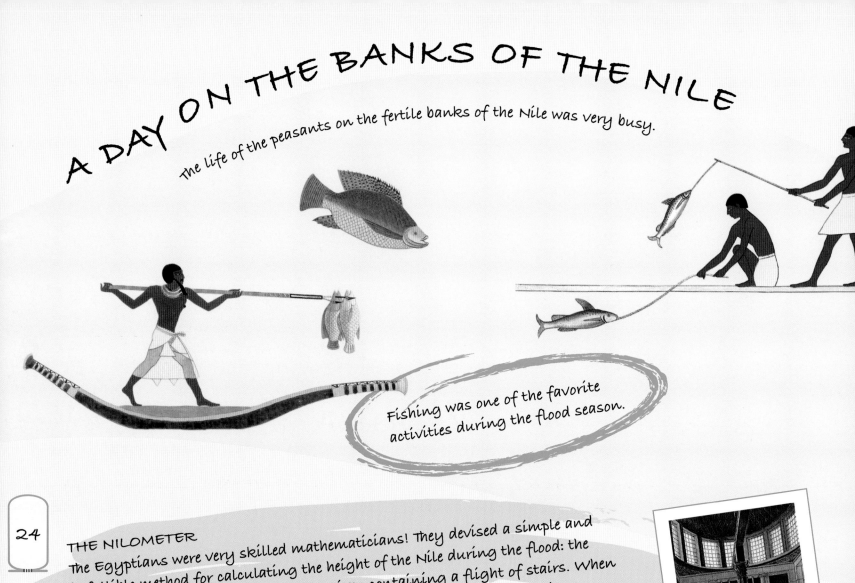

Fishing was one of the favorite activities during the flood season.

THE NILOMETER

The Egyptians were very skilled mathematicians! They devised a simple and infallible method for calculating the height of the Nile during the flood: the Nilometer. Wells were dug close to the river, containing a flight of stairs. When the level of the Nile rose, the water reached the highest steps. The Egyptians calculated the extent of the flood by counting how many stairs the water covered.

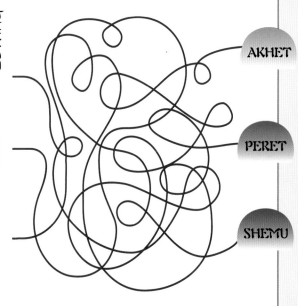

AKHET, PERET AND SHEMU

THE FLOODING OF THE NILE WAS SO IMPORTANT THAT IT INFLUENCED ALL ASPECTS OF EGYPTIAN LIFE, INCLUDING THE CALENDAR, WHICH WAS ACTUALLY BASED ON THE OBSERVATION OF THE RIVER! THE EGYPTIANS DIVIDED THE YEAR INTO THREE SEASONS OF FOUR MONTHS EACH. THE FIRST CORRESPONDED TO THE FLOODING OF THE FIELDS, THE SECOND TO THE SOWING SEASON AND THE THIRD TO THE HARVEST. LINK THE PEASANTS' ACTIVITIES TO THE PERIOD DURING WHICH THEY WERE PERFORMED TO DISCOVER THE NAMES OF THE THREE EGYPTIAN SEASONS.

SOWING

FLOOD

HARVEST

AKHET

PERET

SHEMU

In the countryside, instead of guard dogs the peasants kept baboons, which they also trained to pick fruit!

Goats, sheep and chickens were raised on the farms, but the most important animals were cows. Owning lots of livestock was a sign of wealth.

Grapes were also grown in the Nile Delta. The wine obtained by crushing the fruit was reserved for the most sumptuous and refined banquets.

THE DOG, THE GOOSE AND THE SACK OF GRAIN

ABU, A YOUNG PEASANT, MUST CARRY A DOG, A GOOSE, AND A SACK OF GRAIN TO THE OPPOSITE BANK OF THE NILE, BUT HIS LITTLE PAPYRUS BOAT CAN ONLY TRANSPORT ONE OF THEM AT A TIME. IF ABU TAKES THE GRAIN, LEAVING THE DOG ALONE WITH THE GOOSE, THE DOG WILL ATTACK IT. HOWEVER, IF HE LEAVES THE GOOSE WITH THE GRAIN, THE BIRD WILL EAT IT. WHAT SHOULD HE DO? HELP ABU TO FIND A WAY TO CARRY THE GRAIN, THE DOG AND THE GOOSE TO THE OPPOSITE BANK OF THE NILE.

KARNAK

Resting on the edge of the basket, Nefer couldn't manage to take his eyes off the view racing beneath them: everything was so familiar and yet so different than when he'd seen it last. Penny was right, he'd find his world just as he'd left it, but all the changes were nonetheless having a strange effect on him. Penny realized and moved closer to him so that he didn't feel lonely. "Is everything all right, Nef?"

"Waset," murmured the little Egyptian.

"What does that mean?" asked Penny.

"It's the Egyptian name of Thebes, my hometown, where the Temple of Karnak stands. We're almost there. Waset means 'the powerful one,'" explained Nefer with a smile, "but Thebes is also called – just a moment, let me think, ah yes! – 'the center of the world, the queen of cities, the divine…'"

"Wow! It must be magnificent!"

"It sure is! It was the capital of Egypt for centuries and is still the largest and richest city of the entire empire. And the Temple of Karnak is enormous! We call it Ipet-Isut, which means 'the most select of places.' Just think – over 80,000 people work there!"

"How can they? What do all those people do?"

"Well, there are priests – lots of them – but also craftsmen and peasants, who don't work in the temple, of course, but in the fields belonging to the temple. Karnak even commands a fleet of over 80 ships!"

Alex whistled in wonder. "How do you know all these things?"

"Didn't I tell you? My father's a scribe, one of the officials. I know the temple like the back of my hand. I've been everywhere," boasted Nefer and then, checking that Penny wasn't listening, whispered to Alex, "and I mean everywhere! Even the rooms that are strictly off-limits! I must tell you about a couple of tricks that I've used to distract the priests!"

"Nef my friend, I think you and I need to talk!" answered Alex with a grin.

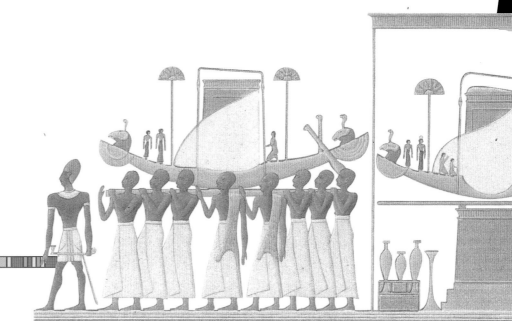

EXPLORE THE TEMPLE OF KARNAK WITH NEFER

The scarab is hidden in the most sacred part of the Temple of Karnak: the sanctuary, which is the room that houses the statue of the god. At dawn, noon and evening each day, the high priest enters the room to present the god with offerings of food, drink and perfumed incense. The statue is then undressed, washed and dressed in clean linen clothes. These rituals are performed to entice the god to inhabit the statue and consequently, the temple. Of course, nobody except the pharaoh and the most important priests can enter, but you're lucky: I know this place like the back of my hand and I've got a plan! Are you ready for a mission impossible? Off we go!

STAGE ONE: THE APPROACH!

High walls surround the temple, giving it an imposing appearance similar to a fortress. How can we solve this problem? Easy: by proceeding to Stage Two!

STAGE TWO: ENTRY!

The temple can be entered through the entrance gate. It's easy to find, as it's flanked by two towers, known as a pylon, in front of which two obelisks usually stood. The pylon leads onto a huge courtyard.

STAGE THREE: WATCH OUT FOR THE PRIESTS!

The priests can be recognized by their leopard-skin cloaks.

We must be careful, as we're near the sacred lake, where we could easily bump into the priests. Why's that? Let me explain. Nobody can disturb the god in his chamber and the few priests permitted to enter the most sacred part of the temple must purify themselves by shaving their head and body and washing many times a day. Only the water of the sacred lake, near the temple walls, can be used for this purpose.

Hypostyle is a Greek term that means "resting upon pillars."
Crossing the central courtyard will take you to the entrance of the Great Hypostyle Hall. This is a huge hall that must be crossed to reach the sanctuary. Of course, the entrance is not open to everyone, so we must hide, but it's not difficult! The Hypostyle Hall resembles a maze because it's supported by 134 pillars. The great room is enveloped in semidarkness because the daylight only enters through a few small windows near the ceiling. The columns resemble papyrus plants, with a long stem and a flower at the top.

The Hypostyle Hall

THE HYPOSTYLE HALL IS A MAZE!

Cross the Hypostyle Hall to reach the sanctuary where the scarab is hidden.

THE MYSTERY OF THE SCARAB

JOIN THE DOTS FROM 1 TO 55 TO
DISCOVER YOUR NEXT DESTINATION.

LUXOR

The Temple of Luxor, seen from above: look how small the boats seem in comparison!

"It's sooooo hot!" Alex complained.

"Don't interrupt me, Alex. Just listen. This is very interesting: Misterius' guidebook says that the temples of Karnak and Luxor are two of the most important in Egypt and that they're both in Thebes, and…"

"Penny, it's too hot for that book! It's so hot! Let's wait for Nefer to join us. He'll tell us where we need to go. Let's wait here in the shade of this sphinx."

Penny cast a dirty look at her brother. "Nef will be here any minute. I'm just trying to interpret those strange signs that we found on the back of the scarab. And on the subject of that sphinx, the two temples are linked by an avenue flanked by granite sphinxes…"

"Which sphinx have we reached?" Alex interrupted again, making a big show of wiping the sweat from his forehead with a corner of his shirt.

Penny raised her eyes from the book, exasperated. "The eighth. You don't need to be a genius at math to count the sphinxes behind us! How come you're complaining so much?"

"Because I'm melting! It's incredibly hot here!"

Nefer and Mew joined them. "Hey Alex, you're all sweaty! Are you hot?"

Alex didn't feel like answering him, especially after having noticed that the young Egyptian looked cool and rested, despite having run to meet them and the temperature of over 100 degrees and the sun beating fiercely down on their heads. Mew didn't seem hot either, and kept jumping from one sphinx to another, apparently having a great time and overjoyed to be back on the ground rather than up in the sky in the hot air balloon.

"Have you discovered anything, Nef?" asked Penny.

"Nothing at all. Those signs are a mystery! They look like graffiti, but there are no clues in the hieroglyphs that I stopped to read," answered Nef thoughtfully. "I can't wait to compare them with those engraved on the back of the next scarab. Is it much further?"

"We're only at the eighth sphinx," murmured Alex, dejectedly.

"It seems as though you and the mighty Ra don't get along too well!" laughed Nefer.

"Ra? Who's he?"

"The sun god! One of the most important Egyptian gods!" replied Nef, looking at him unbelievingly. "Do you at least know who Amen and Isis are?"

"Um, more or less…"

"I can't believe it! Let's go, friend, and I'll tell you how the gods and the world were born."

THE CREATION OF THE WORLD

According to the legend, at the beginning of time the world was covered by an ocean called Nun. One day a hill emerged from Nun.

Atum, the god of creation, reached the hill and gave life to the first two gods – with a sneeze!

Here's Shu, the god of the air, and Tefnut, the goddess of moisture, whose name means "Atum's saliva!"

The offspring of Shu and Tefnut were Nut, the goddess of the sky, and Gheb, the god of the earth, who in turn became the parents of…

…Nephthys, Osiris, the first ruler of Egypt, his wife Isis, and Set, the god of chaos, who schemed in the shadow to overthrow his brother. In order to achieve this, Set killed Osiris, who became the god of the underworld. However, Horus, the son of Osiris and Isis, decided to avenge his father's death and challenged Set!

HORUS VS. SET

Here are this evening's challengers!
On your left, Horus, the falcon-headed god, son of
Isis and Osiris, the god of the sky and the rising
sun. On your right, Set, the god resembling an
imaginary animal, brother of Osiris and uncle of
Horus, the god of chaos, storms and disorder. Horus
has challenged Set to avenge his father's death and
to prevent his divine uncle from ruling the world and
reducing it to chaos and darkness. The moment
of the final round has come, but Set doesn't seem
worried by Horus' threats, and I can't believe my eyes!
Set is laughing, which is making the falcon-headed god more
furious than ever! It's dangerous – very dangerous – to anger a
god. And look! Horus has launched a surprise attack and knocked
Set down. The fight is on! It's immediately clear that there are no
holds barred. And when two gods fight without rules, absolutely
anything is possible! It's impossible to describe what's happening
here! A series of attacks and defensive moves, followed by
counterattacks, and now Horus is on the floor! The sun god
is on the floor! Just a moment! Horus has leapt back to
his feet and is fighting back! He's very fast and
completely out of control! Set can do nothing to stop his
attack, and it's a knockout after just two moves. The god of
chaos is unable to get up, but tries a last desperate move,
turning over and striking out at Horus' eye! The sky god is
injured! But the fight is over: Set has been defeated and Horus
is the winner!

HORUS' EYE

Ever since the day of his victory over the evil Set, Horus' injured eye
was considered a powerful talisman. The ancient Egyptians snapped
up his amulets! Almost everyone wore these little objects as lucky
charms, and hundreds of them were inserted between the bandages of mummies. Their power was
derived from both the material from which they were made – lapis lazuli, pottery, gold or silver –
and from their shape. Each amulet had a specific meaning: the scarab was a symbol of change,
the eye of Horus (known as *udjat*) had exceptional healing properties, while those seeking good
luck chose the ankh, the cross that symbolized power and eternal life.

THE EGYPTIAN GODS

The ancient Egyptians worshipped over 2000 gods! However, some of these were more important than others and were familiar and venerated throughout the country. They were believed to protect Egypt and the most important activities of daily life. The gods were often represented as animals or with the head of animals that became the symbol of their powers.

Discover the powers and distinctive features of some of the most important Egyptian deities.

RA

POWER: THE SUN GOD
DISTINCTIVE FEATURES: A FALCON'S HEAD TOPPED BY THE SUN DISK.

SIGNATURE

THOTH

POWER: THE GOD OF WRITING
DISTINCTIVE FEATURES: AN IBIS' HEAD. HE CAN ALSO CHANGE INTO A BABOON.

SIGNATURE

SEKHMET

POWER: THE GODDESS OF WAR
DISTINCTIVE FEATURES: A LIONESS' HEAD.

SIGNATURE

ONE VERY POPULAR DEITY WAS DEPICTED AS A CAT. SHE PROTECTED HOUSES AND BROUGHT PEACE. THE CITY OF BUBASTIS HAS A TEMPLE DEDICATED TO HER THAT WAS DECORATED WITH HUNDREDS OF CAT STATUETTES. WHAT'S HER NAME? YOU CAN FIND OUT BY INTERPRETING THE GODS' HANDWRITING: LINK EACH "SIGNATURE" WITH THE NAME OF THE GOD THAT IT REPRESENTS AND WRITE IT IN THE CORRESPONDING SQUARES. AT THE END OF THE GAME, THE HIGHLIGHTED SQUARES WILL SHOW THE NAME OF THE CAT GODDESS.

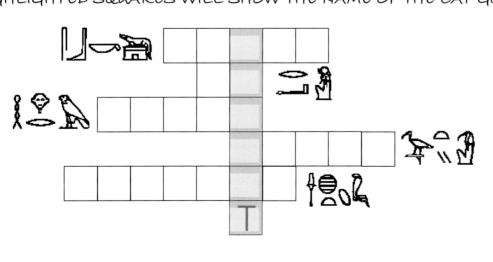

HORUS

POWER: THE PROTECTOR OF THE PHARAOH, OFTEN KNOWN AS THE "LIVING HORUS"

DISTINCTIVE FEATURES: HE TURNS INTO A FALCON.

SIGNATURE

SOBEK

POWER: THE GOD OF WATER

DISTINCTIVE FEATURES: A CROCODILE'S HEAD

SIGNATURE

ISIS

POWER: THE MOTHER OF HORUS

DISTINCTIVE FEATURES: A THRONE-SHAPED HEADDRESS

SIGNATURE

THE KEBAB...
...this is the real and amusing meaning of the Greek word "obelisk," as Greek visitors dubbed one of the most imposing and famous monuments of ancient Egypt! An obelisk is a monolith, meaning a single block of stone, with four sides and a pyramidal tip, sometimes covered in gold.

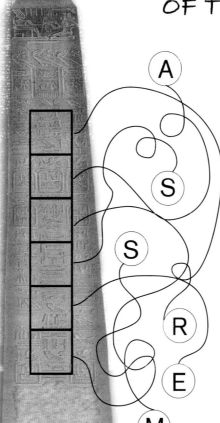

THE MYSTERY OF THE SCARAB

A

S

S

R

E

M

THE NEXT DESTINATION IS THE TEMPLE OF ONE OF THE MOST FAMOUS EGYPTIAN PHARAOHS, WHO WAS SO IMPORTANT AS TO BE CALLED "THE GREAT." DISCOVER HIS NAME BY CARVING THE LETTERS ON THE OBELISK IN THE RIGHT ORDER.

THE RAMESSEUM

Penny pulled the scarab they found in Luxor out of her backpack and examined the strange inscription on its back, as she absentmindedly stroked Mew. "What are you thinking about?" asked Alex, noticing her expression of concentration. "I was wondering what these strange marks engraved on the back of the scarab are for. We probably won't know until we've found all the statues."

"I'm starting to wonder whether we interpreted the last clue correctly and if we're heading for the right place!"

"Don't worry, Alex," interrupted Nefer, "I'm sure it's right. I know the funerary temple of Ramses the Great very well, because it's where I go to school."

The main courtyard of the Ramesseum is home to four colossal statues of Ramses II holding the scepter and the whip, which is actually a royal fly swatter!

"In a funerary temple?" exclaimed the twins, shocked.

"That's right! The Ramesseum is not only a temple, but also has a palace and the 'House of Life,' which is one of the leading schools for scribes. My dad went there too. I think I'm very lucky to have been admitted, because I'll become a scribe! Not just anyone do that!"

"A school!" Alex complained, grunting, "How can you consider yourself lucky because you go to school? And what's it like? As bad as mine?"

"Um, I don't really know. Our teacher is actually quite strict, and always carries a whip, which he uses when we make mistakes."

Alex and Penny looked at each other in amazement.

"You know what, Penny?" blurted Alex, "I never thought I'd say it, but perhaps we're lucky to go to school in the 21st century."

Ramses II was one of the greatest and longest-living pharaohs in Egyptian history. He ruled for 66 years!

DID YOU KNOW?

The pharaoh was considered a living god represented by the god Horus, and was thus worshipped and feared by the people. He ruled Egypt and was the high priest and the head of the armies. The figure of the pharaoh can be recognized by the symbols of royalty worn by the sovereign: two crowns, one red and one white, a cobra on his forehead, a blue and white striped headdress, the royal beard, two scepters and a bull's tail that he wore hanging from his belt.

THE HOUSE OF LIFE
Let's visit an ancient Egyptian school with Nefer

The House of Life is a place where many boys study to become scribes like my dad. Scribes play a very important role in Egyptian society, as they are the only people who learn to read and write. Indeed, learning to use hieroglyphs is no easy task, for this writing system is composed of over 6000 symbols, each of which is not a letter, like in the alphabet, but a drawing that expresses an idea.

A SCRIBE'S TABLET

Each scribe always carries a tool to flatten the papyrus and a case containing all his writing implements: reed pens, dry ink and water to dilute it.

THE HIEROGLYPHS

Hieroglyphs can be written from right to left, but also in the opposite direction, or even from top to bottom! It's all very confusing!

These complicated symbols are sacred and are chiefly used for inscriptions in tombs or temples, while a simpler and quicker system, known as hieratic writing, is used for everyday purposes.

HOW TO MAKE A PAPYRUS

The thin outer membrane of the papyrus stalks is removed and the stalks are cut into narrow strips. These strips are wetted, arranged in two overlapping layers and pressed well. The strips stick firmly together as they dry, forming a dark sheet of material that is stiff but strong.

I've often watched my dad working and I've noticed that he always sits cross-legged and spreads the papyrus on his knees before starting to write. He then takes a reed from his case, cuts the tip, and moistens it with water to soften the ink. After having sprinkled a few drops on the sheet to honor Thoth, the god of writing, my dad is ready to work.

THE MYSTERY OF THE HIEROGLYPHS

The ability to interpret the complex hieroglyphs was lost over the centuries, and gradually they became meaningless signs. They might have remained mysterious symbols forever if it weren't for a stone slab and a French genius who knew ancient Greek. This is the story of how the mystery of the hieroglyphs was solved.

THE ROSETTA STONE

The Rosetta Stone is a large and not particularly attractive slab of black stone. It was discovered in the desert by Napoleon's troops in 1799, near a village called Rosetta. So what makes this simple object the most important find in the history of Egyptology? The fact that it was incised with the same text in three different languages: ancient Greek, demotic (a script similar to hieratic writing) and hieroglyphs.

The stone was the key to understanding hieroglyphs, but a very smart guy was needed to use it....

Jean François Champollion had a real passion for languages! At the age of 16 he already knew Latin, Hebrew, Syriac, Arabic and Chinese, but it was his knowledge of ancient Greek that gave him an important insight: he understood that it was possible to compare the Greek text on the Rosetta Stone with the ancient Egyptian writing, starting with a word that was undoubtedly the same in both languages: the pharaoh's name.

Champollion discovered that the rulers' names in the hieroglyphic text are written in frames similar to those of comic strips, known as "cartouches".

By studying the cartouches, he was able to discover the rules for interpreting the hieroglyphs and reading a form or writing that nobody had used for over 1400 years!

THE MYSTERY OF THE SCARAB

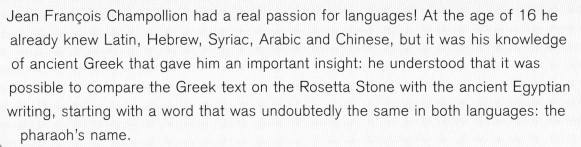

EPLSIUSTK ➡ PYTLHE
UTMSNSHOBE ONTSSTEATUM
ALUTMSNSHOBE ELSGEOODSFHCOA

CROSS OUT THE LETTERS OF THE WORDS LISTED. READ THE REMAINING LETTERS OF THE CARTOUCHE IN SEQUENCE TO DISCOVER WHERE THE NEXT SCARAB IS HIDDEN.

PYLONS – STATUES – GODS – COLUMNS – OBELISK

THE COLOSSI OF MEMNON

Penny was very worried about Mew. Each time the cat traveled in the hot air balloon, she seemed to lose all trace of the proverbial feline sense of balance and started to stagger from side to side of the basket, covering her face with her paws and assuming the sorriest expression the girl had ever seen. Can cats suffer from airsickness? A look at Mew convinced Penny that it was indeed possible!

"Nef, do you think Mew is all right?"

"Actually, I've never seen her look so unhappy, except when we have to travel on the Nile.... Alex, perhaps it would be best to stop and let her out for a few minutes."

"Oh come on! Cats don't suffer from airsickness!"

"But what if they do? Mew would get sick in 'your' balloon," Penny pointed out.

"Are you sure you want to run the risk?"

"We'll land right away!! I'll touch down over there, near those two statues. The onboard computer calls them the Colossi of Memnon, and they really do look enormous! Nef, what can you tell us about those statues?"

"Nothing! There aren't any statues with that name, and right in the middle of the desert to boot!"

"Perhaps they've been moved for some mysterious reason."

"Right! Or perhaps..."

"Hold on a minute! Here's the answer to the mystery," Penny interrupted, after having consulted Misterius' guidebook. "That was the ancient Greek name for the statues."

"Wouldn't you just know that the Greeks had something to do with it? Here too! They're persecuting me!"

"Shut up, Alex! Memnon was the name of a mythical African prince, but the statues actually depict a pharaoh, Amenhotep III."

"Just a sec! Of course! Those two statues stood at the entrance of the Temple of Amenhotep! Come on, let's land near the statues. You have to see them close up, they're absolutely huge!"

The Temple of Amenhotep III was built so that it would be submerged when the Nile flooded. When the waters retreated, the walls of the temple reappeared, symbolizing the rebirth of the fields. Unfortunately, this unusual feature was one of the causes of destruction of the temple, which gradually crumbled away.

DEIR EL-BAHARI

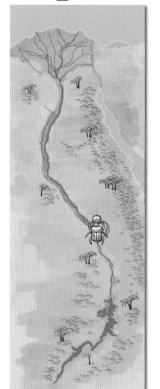

"Meowwwww!"

"Nef, say something to your cat and make her get off the button of the supersonic engines immediately!"

"Sorry, Alex," said Nefer, moving the cat off the onboard computer, "she's always jumpy when we fly."

"Meowww!"

"Stay still, Mew! Look down there: we're here, that's Deir el-Bahari."

Penny leaned out to take a look and the view took her breath away. "It's beautiful! Come and take a look, Alex!"

"I can't, Penny, I have to land Epsilon. Where do you want to touch down?"

"Meoww…"

"Mew, stay still! The temple is composed of three terraces linked by steps, see? Let's land on the first flight, so that I can tell you the story of Hatshepsut, the woman who became pharaoh, while we climb up to the temple."

But Nefer didn't have time to start telling the story, because as soon as the balloon touched down, Mew leapt from her master's arms and ran inside the temple.

"Mew!!!"

44

The children ran up the three terraces after her.

"Mew," called Nefer, peeking inside the temple, "where are you???"

"Whew, that cat will have me to answer to!" threatened Alex breathlessly.

"Wait!" yelled Penny, rummaging through her backpack and bringing out a flashlight. "There she is! And look what she's sitting on!" Penny turned the flashlight onto Mew, who was washing her fur, sat peacefully on the scarab!

DID YOU KNOW?

Take a good look at this portrait of Hatshepsut, and you'll notice that the queen has a beard! The pharaohs always wore a wooden beard, fastened with a cord. This attribute was the symbol of the ruler's divine nature, and was thus also worn by women pharaohs!

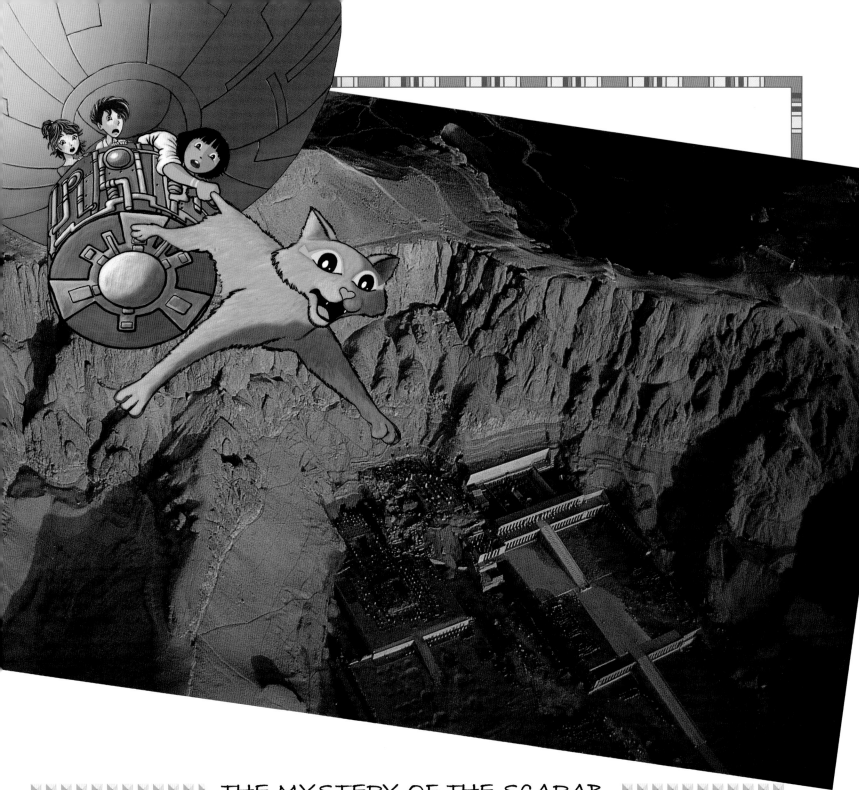

THE MYSTERY OF THE SCARAB

REPLACE EACH NUMBER WITH THE CORRESPONDING
LETTER OF THE ALPHABET TO DISCOVER THE NEXT
DESTINATION.

EXAMPLE

A = 1   4   5   9   18   5   12   13   5   4   9   14   1

B = 2

C = 3   ....

DEIR EL-MEDINA

A light started flashing on the hot air balloon's onboard computer and Alex hurried to read the information on the screen.

"Hey guys, according to Epsilon, we're almost there."

"But there must be something wrong," said Penny, after leaning out of the basket. "I can't see any village. What about you, Nef?"

"I can't either, but this is the right place, I recognize those hills!"

"Do you mean you've been here before?" asked Penny.

"Oh yes! My father worked as a scribe in Deir el-Medina and I lived here with my family for a while. It was great! This is a very special village that is home to the workers who build and decorate the nearby tombs of the pharaohs, in the Valley of the Kings."

"So the painters lived here too?" asked Penny, enthusiastic about the idea of seeing the places where the colorful Egyptian frescoes were painted.

"That's right! And the very best ones at that! And also the sculptors, potters, carpenters, glassmakers and jewelers!"

"WOW! I wish I could have seen them at work!

"Well, it wouldn't have been easy, even in my day! There were guards everywhere to protect the artists and their works. In order to enter Deir el-Medina, you had to pass roadblocks and checkpoints at the gates of the village, which was surrounded by a high wall. The workers were also organized like an army: my father told me that they were divided into teams, each headed by a foreman who directed the work. However, life here was not bad at all: the white houses had their own small courtyards. We also had a terrace, with a view over the entire village, with identical little houses, perfectly straight roads and palm trees. Try picturing it...."

The outer wall and a few traces of the houses are all that remain of the ancient craftsmen's village.

CRAFTSMEN AT WORK

Craftsmen were highly respected in ancient Egypt, but it was not easy to join their ranks. It was necessary to work hard and learn how to use special tools, like the ones depicted in this fresco.

The axe was one of the most common tools in ancient Egypt. The carpenters used axes to shape the wooden planks used to make furniture.

Saws had bronze blades. This tool, almost identical to its modern counterpart, was used to cut the wooden planks.

The mallet was a wooden hammer. It was used with a chisel to carve wood or stone.

The craftsmen worked for hours seated on little wooden stools. Do you think they were comfortable?

This strange drill was used to bore holes in wood.

TO EACH HIS OWN

Discover who these three craftsmen are and what they are creating by connecting each to his work.

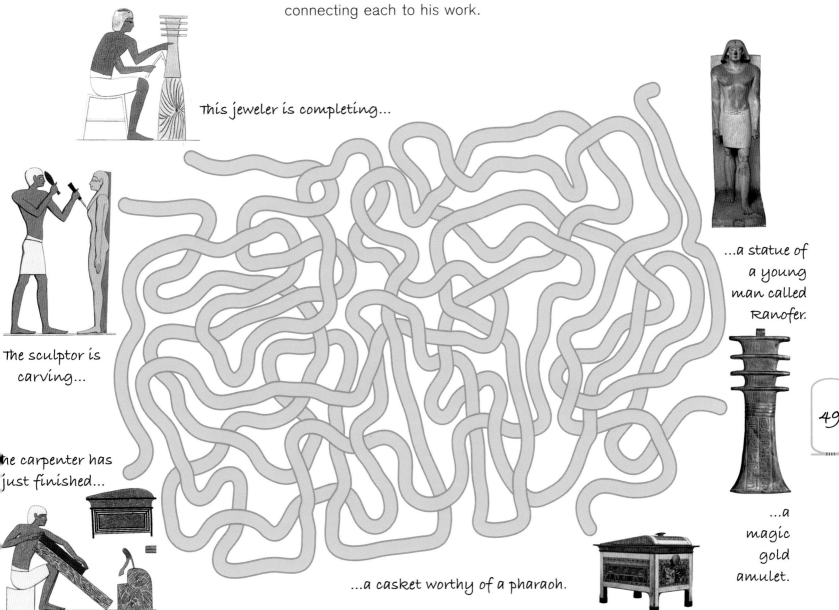

This jeweler is completing...

...a statue of a young man called Ranofer.

The sculptor is carving...

The carpenter has just finished...

...a casket worthy of a pharaoh.

...a magic gold amulet.

THE MYSTERY OF THE SCARAB

IN ORDER TO FIND THE NEXT SCARAB, YOU MUST PROVE YOUR COURAGE AND ENTER THE TOMB OF ONE OF EGYPT'S GREATEST PHARAOHS. REPLACE EACH SYMBOL WITH THE CORRESPONDING LETTER TO DISCOVER WHERE IT IS HIDDEN. WHEN YOU HAVE FINISHED, READ THE SOLUTION AND GET READY TO ENTER THE TOMB OF...

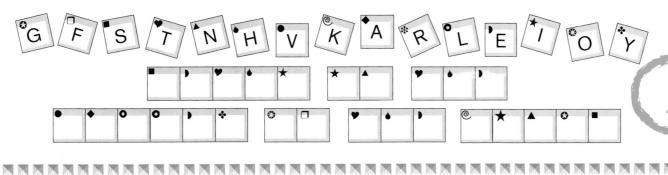

G F S T N H V K A R L E I O Y

"No, no and no! I can't enter the Valley of the Kings or the Valley of the Queens, and I'd certainly NEVER enter a pharaoh's tomb. It's forbidden! It's the most forbidden thing of all!!"

"Nef, my friend, you have to come."

"Alex, there's no way!"

"But Nef..."

"Meow!"

"Did you hear that, Penny? Mew agrees with me too!"

"Nef, we don't understand! Can you explain why the Valley of the Kings and the Valley of the Queens are so sacred?"

"This is the burial place of countless pharaohs, queens and nobles."

"Well, I can't see anything," muttered Alex, perplexed, "so where are all these tombs?"

DID YOU KNOW?
For 500 years, from 1552 BC, pharaohs and noblemen chose to carve their tombs out of the rock in the impenetrable Valley of the Kings in an attempt to protect their rest and their treasures from the greed of tomb robbers. So far archeologists have found the tombs of 62 sovereigns and noblemen in the Valley of the Kings. Who knows how many discoveries remain to be made in the great royal necropolis?

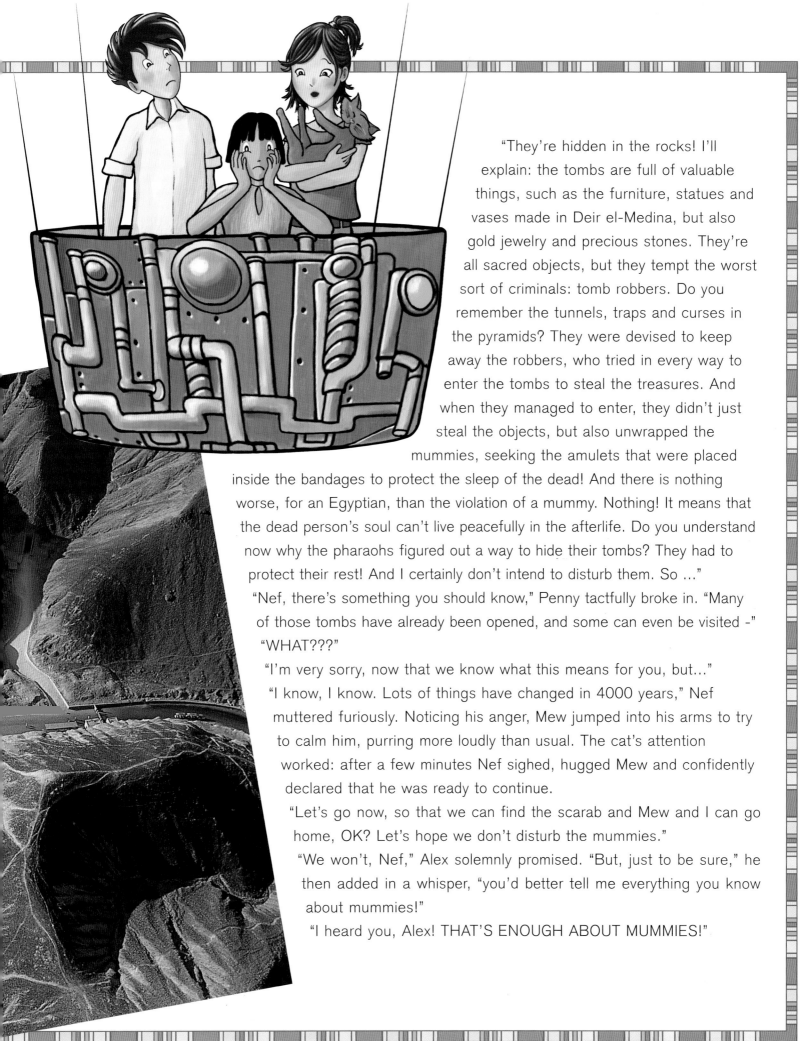

"They're hidden in the rocks! I'll explain: the tombs are full of valuable things, such as the furniture, statues and vases made in Deir el-Medina, but also gold jewelry and precious stones. They're all sacred objects, but they tempt the worst sort of criminals: tomb robbers. Do you remember the tunnels, traps and curses in the pyramids? They were devised to keep away the robbers, who tried in every way to enter the tombs to steal the treasures. And when they managed to enter, they didn't just steal the objects, but also unwrapped the mummies, seeking the amulets that were placed inside the bandages to protect the sleep of the dead! And there is nothing worse, for an Egyptian, than the violation of a mummy. Nothing! It means that the dead person's soul can't live peacefully in the afterlife. Do you understand now why the pharaohs figured out a way to hide their tombs? They had to protect their rest! And I certainly don't intend to disturb them. So ..."

"Nef, there's something you should know," Penny tactfully broke in. "Many of those tombs have already been opened, and some can even be visited -"

"WHAT???"

"I'm very sorry, now that we know what this means for you, but..."

"I know, I know. Lots of things have changed in 4000 years," Nef muttered furiously. Noticing his anger, Mew jumped into his arms to try to calm him, purring more loudly than usual. The cat's attention worked: after a few minutes Nef sighed, hugged Mew and confidently declared that he was ready to continue.

"Let's go now, so that we can find the scarab and Mew and I can go home, OK? Let's hope we don't disturb the mummies."

"We won't, Nef," Alex solemnly promised. "But, just to be sure," he then added in a whisper, "you'd better tell me everything you know about mummies!"

"I heard you, Alex! THAT'S ENOUGH ABOUT MUMMIES!"

THE SECRETS OF THE MUMMIES

The Egyptians believed that after death the soul would return to the body and its owner would be able to return to life in the afterworld. However, this would only be possible if the body remained intact. Consequently, they specialized in a very special embalming technique.

Do you want to know all the secrets of the Egyptian mummies?

Secret 1

Not all mummies are Egyptian! The mummmification of a body – a person or an animal – is a process that can also occur naturally in cold places, such as a glacier, or hot dry places, such as a desert. In fact, the first Egyptian mummies were simply bodies buried in the scorching desert sand.

Secret 2

Anubis is the embalming god. Anubis really was present during the process of mummification, for one of the priests wore a mask representing the jackal-headed god.

Secret 3

Do you know what the word "mummy" means? Wax! When the Arabs conquered Egypt they found the first mummies, whose bandages were sealed with a dark resin. Misunderstanding the nature of this resin, the Arabs called the bandaged bodies *mummiya*, the Arabic word for "wax."

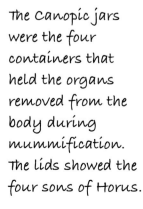

The Canopic jars were the four containers that held the organs removed from the body during mummification. The lids showed the four sons of Horus.

MUMMIFICATION ACCORDING TO NEFER

Are you ready, Alex? I'll explain the mummification process to you. First of all the embalming priests remove the brain through the nose and extract the internal organs, except the heart. The liver, lungs, stomach and intestines are placed in special urns called Canopic jars. The body is then covered with *natron*, a crystallized salt, and left to dry for 40 days. Many yards of linen bandages are then wrapped around the body. To protect the mummy, the priests hide hundreds of amulets between the layers of bandages the mummy. The body is now ready to be buried. A mask is placed over the face and the mummy is transferred to a sarcophagus. Seventy days have passed since death.

Animals were mummified too! After death certain sacred animals, such as cats, crocodiles and baboons were embalmed in order to allow them to continue living in the afterworld. Hundreds of cat mummies were buried in Bubasti, the sacred city of the goddess Bastet.

THE BOOK OF THE DEAD... IS NOT FRIGHTENING!

Before reaching the afterlife, the soul of the dead person, called the *ba*, had to cross the underworld, which was a dark and dangerous place! It was inhabited by snakes, crocodiles and evil spirits, which could only be overcome by magic spells. These useful spells were collected in a "guide to the underworld" called the "Book of the Dead." The essential rolls of papyrus bearing the text of the Book of the Dead were placed in the sarcophagus, or even wrapped around the mummy like a bandage.

WEIGHING THE HEART

After having dealt with the dangers of the underworld, the ba had to face one last test: the weighing of the heart. The heart of the dead person was placed on the plate of a scale in the presence of Osiris, the god of the afterworld. Its weight was compared with that of the feather of Maat, the goddess of justice. The outcome was unpredictable: if the person had behaved fairly during life, his heart would be as light as a feather, but if he had been evil, his heart would be weighed down with the wrongs that he had committed and would fall off the scale into the jaws of Sobek, the crocodile god. Thoth recorded the scene impartially, but Anubis would often lean on the scale to make it tip in favor of the dead: the test was passed, and the ba was safe and could finally enter the afterworld!

THE TOMB OF SETHI I

Are you absolutely sure that we can enter the tomb of the great Sethi? What about the pharaoh's curse?"

"Nefer, we've already discussed it. We have to enter to find the scarab. Ouch! Be careful, Alex!"

"Sorry, Penny, but I can't see a thing in the dark!"

"I'll look for the flashlight."

DID YOU KNOW?

Giovanni Battista Belzoni was an Italian adventurer and explorer nicknamed "the Giant" due to his huge size. During the early 1800s, the Giant discovered and excavated dozens of tombs, including those of six pharaohs and the temple of Abu Simbel. He was the first to enter the tomb of Sethi I in over 4000 years and in his diary he described its splendid decorations, in which even the hieroglyphs were colored.

Giovanni Battista Belzoni

"Shouldn't we discuss the curses first?"
"Darn! How many times do I have to tell you? We're not the first ones to enter and those who have been here before us have never been harmed by any strange curse, so stop making such a fuss, scaredy-cat! Here's the flashlight. Now, I'll switch it on and…"
"OOOOOOH!"

The portrait of Sethi I

The children were lost for words when they saw what the flashlight had revealed: they were standing in a brightly colored room, decorated with hundreds of figures of different sizes. And they were even more amazed when they raised their eyes, for the blue-painted ceiling was covered with thousands of figures and little golden stars. The effect was incredible: just like being beneath a starry sky!
"Meow!" The cat impatiently reminded them that they had a mission to accomplish.
"Mew's right, guys, let's go!" Nefer walked behind Mew, followed by Alex, while Penny was unable to take her eyes off the scene painted on a nearby column. She was already looking for her sketchbook in her backpack when Nef went back to find her.
"No, Penny! We haven't got time!"
"Nef, I'm just going to draw this tiny detail, I want to remember the exact shade of this blue and –"
"Will you give up the idea if I tell you how the painters worked? I know because I saw them doing it millions of times, remember?"
"OK! But I want to know everything: how did they make the colors? And why are people always depicted in profile? And were their brushes like mine? And… Nef, wait for me!"
"DARN!"

WARNING: WET PAINT!

Are you as curious as Penny to know how the Egyptians painted? Imagine that you are an apprentice decorator at the service of the pharaoh in the Valley of the Kings. Your first task will be to prepare your brushes, which are made from palm fibers. You can crush or chew the tips to give them the desired shape, as you prefer.

Don't forget the paint: to make the colors, you mix egg white with several natural substances – charcoal for black and chalk for white, for example. If you need yellow or orange, then you must find colored earth, such as ocher.

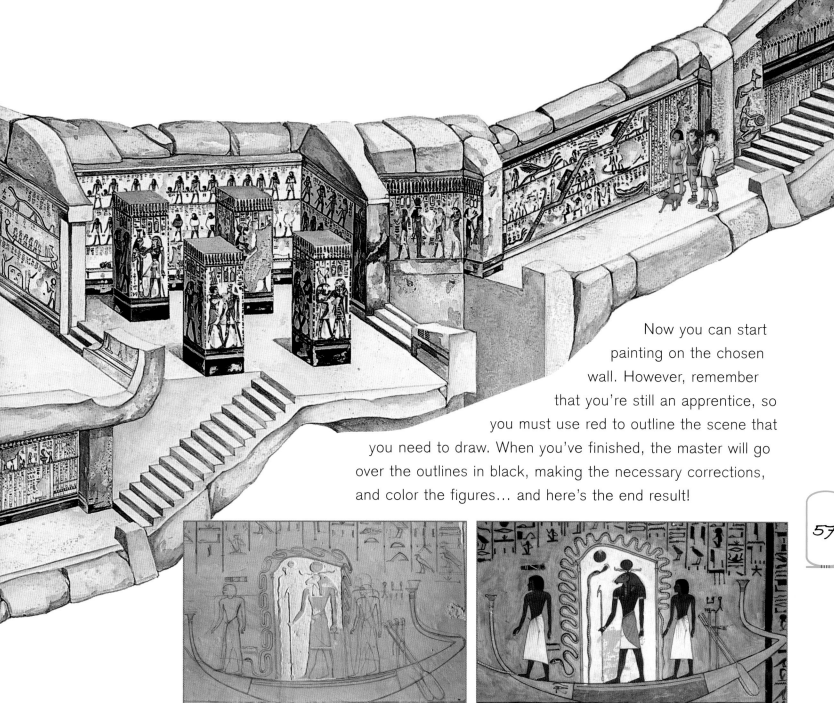

Now you can start painting on the chosen wall. However, remember that you're still an apprentice, so you must use red to outline the scene that you need to draw. When you've finished, the master will go over the outlines in black, making the necessary corrections, and color the figures… and here's the end result!

Your sketch

The finished picture

THE MYSTERY OF THE SCARAB

IF YOU CHOOSE THE RIGHT PATH THROUGH THE LETTERS, YOU'LL DISCOVER THE NAME OF ONE OF THE MOST FAMOUS QUEENS OF EGYPT: THE NEXT SCARAB IS HIDDEN IN HER TOMB!

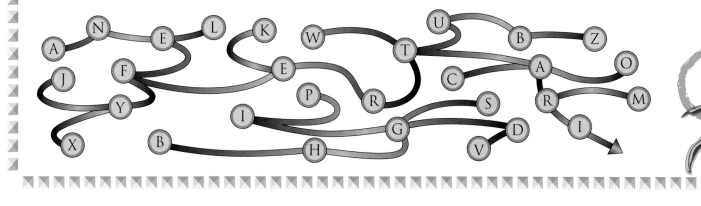

TUTANKHAMEN

Alex would never have admitted it, but he felt more comfortable now that they were out of Sethi's tomb…. Not that he'd been afraid, of course, but breathing the air of the Valley of the Kings made him want to laugh and run and jump.

"Alex, mind the…"

"Agh!!!"

"…steps," finished Penny. "Alex? Are you hurt?" she asked, peering into the tunnel in the rock into which Alex had fallen.

"Hey, come down here! Come take a look!"

Penny and Nefer descended the same steps on which Alex had tripped and joined him in a richly decorated room with a sarcophagus in the middle.

"Nef, read the inscriptions. Whose sarcophagus is this?"

"Let's have a look…. It says Tu… Tut…"

"Tutankhamen!" exclaimed the twins together.

"That's right! But how did you guess?"

"The guide told us about him at that exhibition on the Egyptians," explained Alex, not very helpfully.

"Who? When? Where?"

"I'll explain, Nef," interrupted Penny, realizing that the little Egyptian was more confused than ever. "Tutankhamen ruled Egypt about 3000 years ago. He was still a child, like us, when he became pharaoh. Perhaps you don't know his name because he reign was very short. When he was just 19 years old, the pharaoh…"

Here's a portrait of the boy king.

58

"Was killed! Assassinated by a palace conspiracy!"

"WHAT?!!"

"Alex, you know that has never been proved! Some archeologists believe that the cause of his death was a hunting accident or an illness."

"I think it was a murder at court!"

"OK, Sherlock Holmes, if that's what you want to think. However, Nef should know that in our times Tutankhamen is one of the most famous Egyptian pharaohs, because in 1922 a British archeologist, Howard Carter, discovered his tomb intact, untouched by tomb robbers. When Carter and his patron, Lord Carnarvon, entered the tomb they found a priceless treasure composed of furnishings, statues, jewelry..."

"It sure must have been exciting being the first person to enter a place sealed for thousands of years," Alex commented.

"I think so too! And so did Carter," added Penny, leafing through Misterius' guidebook. "Listen to what he wrote in his diary."

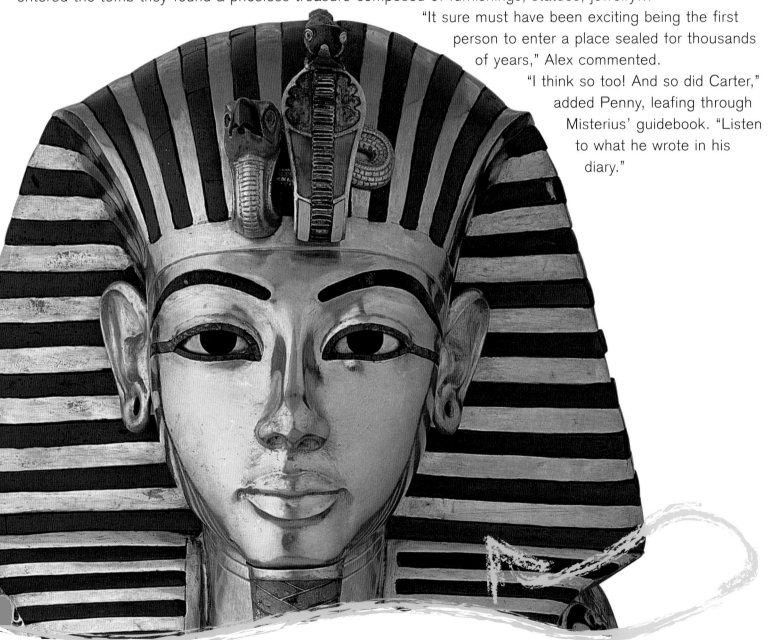

The mask that Carter discovered in Tutankhamen's sarcophagus is one of the most famous objects of antiquity, and certainly also one of the most precious. It is entirely made of gold, while the details of the king's face were created with precious stones.

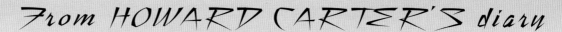

From HOWARD CARTER'S diary

"It was our last period of work in the Valley, where we had dug for six entire seasons, without any results. We were about to give up and leave the Valley to seek better luck elsewhere, when we made a discovery that far exceeded even our wildest dreams."

"It was a thrilling moment for an excavator, quite alone save his native staff of workmen, to suddenly find himself, after so many years of toilsome work."

On 6 November I cabled Lord Carnarvon:

"At last have made wonderful discovery in Valley a magnificent tomb with seals intact recovered same for your arrival congratulations."

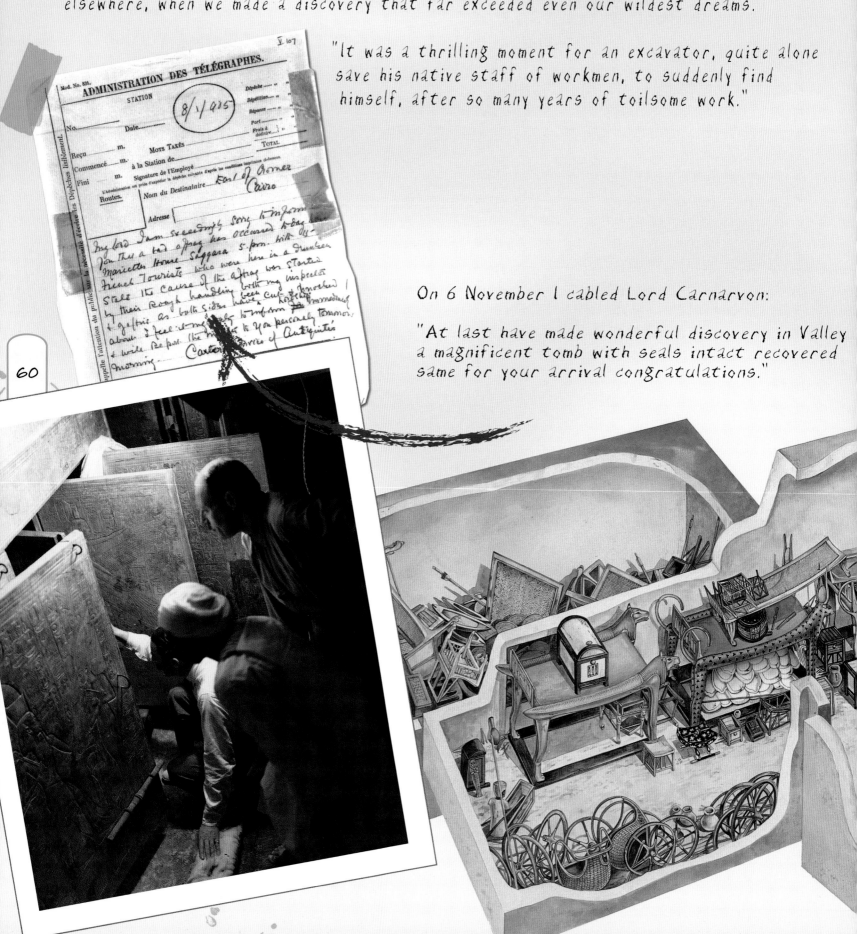

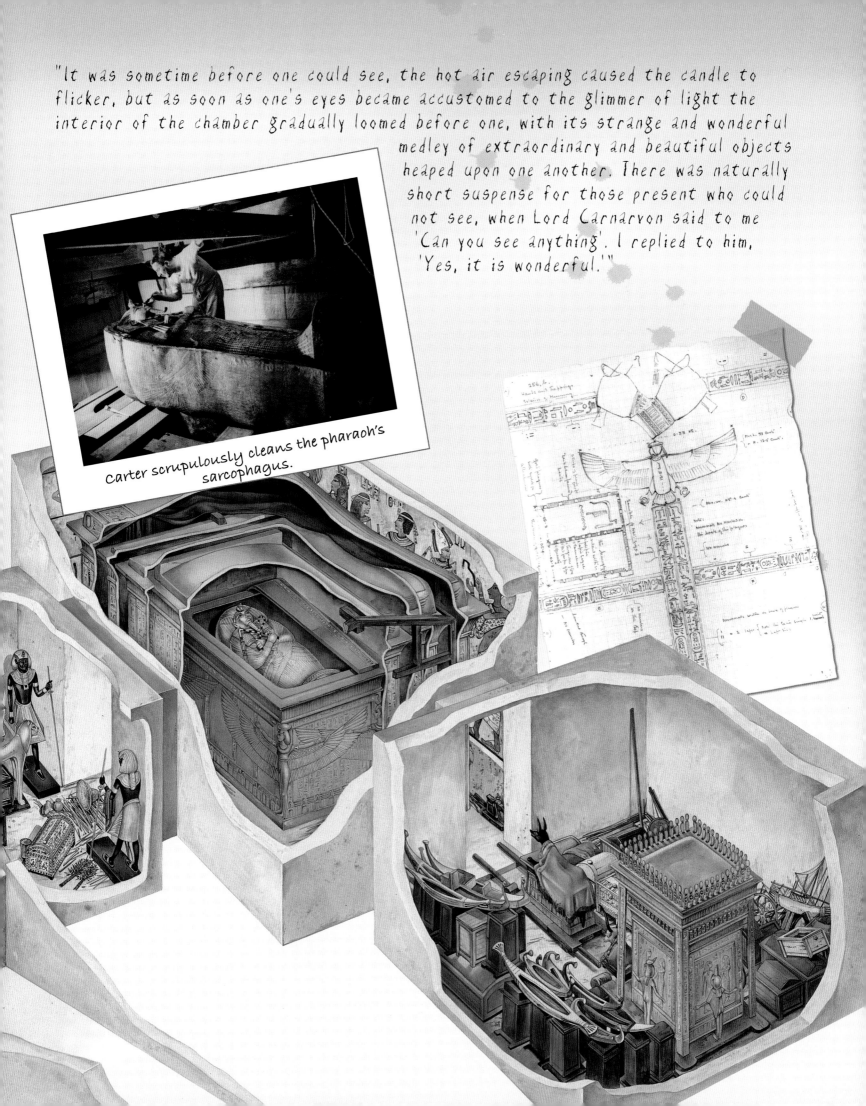

"It was sometime before one could see, the hot air escaping caused the candle to flicker, but as soon as one's eyes became accustomed to the glimmer of light the interior of the chamber gradually loomed before one, with its strange and wonderful medley of extraordinary and beautiful objects heaped upon one another. There was naturally short suspense for those present who could not see, when Lord Carnarvon said to me 'Can you see anything'. I replied to him, 'Yes, it is wonderful.'"

Carter scrupulously cleans the pharaoh's sarcophagus.

A DAY IN THE LIFE OF AN ARCHEOLOGIST

Discover the archeologist in you and enter Tutankhamen's tomb with Carter! Use the colored picture on the previous page to place each object in the exact place where it was found.

The Canopic jars were housed in this gilded shrine.

Three large animal-shaped beds were found.

A statue of the pharaoh, made from gold and ebony (a black wood).

A statue of Anubis crouches on the lid of the casket.

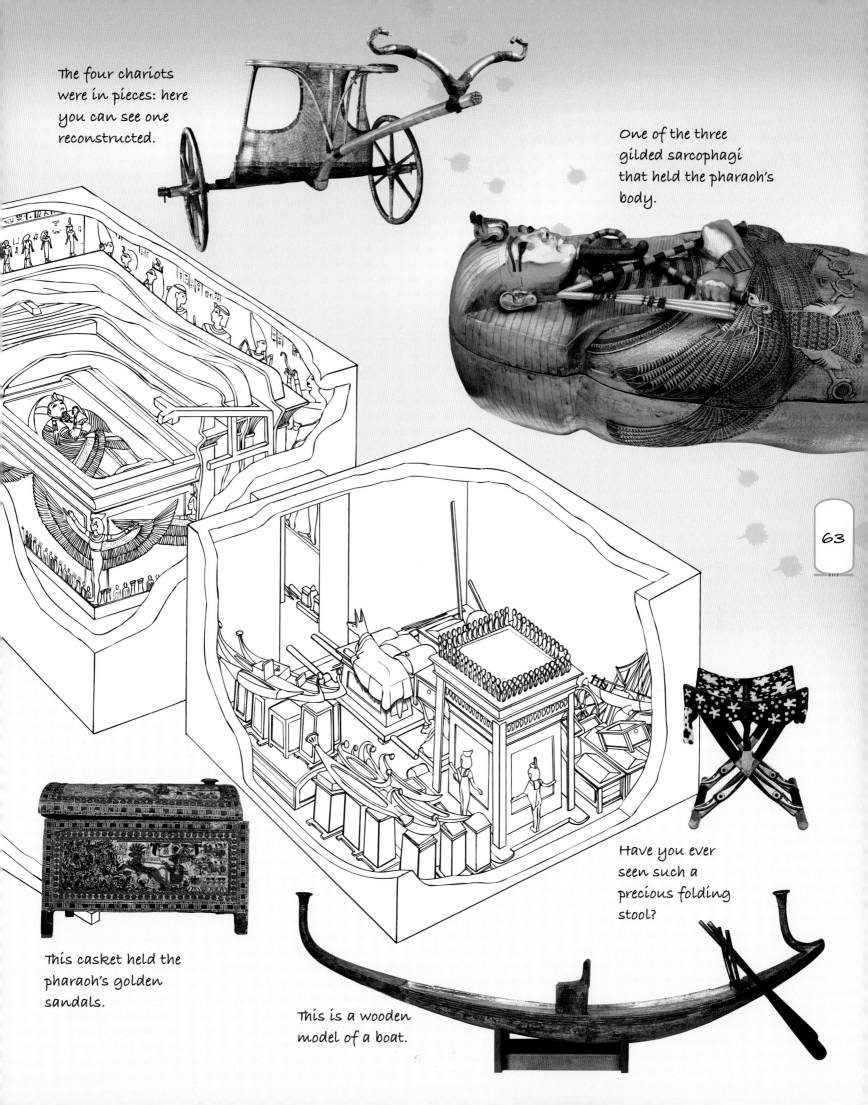

The four chariots were in pieces: here you can see one reconstructed.

One of the three gilded sarcophagi that held the pharaoh's body.

63

Have you ever seen such a precious folding stool?

This casket held the pharaoh's golden sandals.

This is a wooden model of a boat.

NEFERTARI

A brief ride in Epsilon took the children to the Valley of the Queens, the location – according to Nefer – of Nefertari's tomb and the eighth scarab, as well.

While Penny searched her backpack for the flashlight, Alex paced thoughtfully up and down in front of the entrance in the rock.

"Penny, follow my reasoning." he said finally. "If the Egyptian kings were called 'pharaohs,' then the queens were called…"

"Queens," finished Penny, without lifting her head from her backpack.

"Oh, how disappointing…. Oops, I forgot, here's the flashlight, it was in my shirt pocket."

"Alex! You could have told me before! OK, come on Nef and Mew, we can go inside."

"Here we are, Penny!" Nef arrived carrying the little cat. "I'm rather excited, you know…"

"Because we're about to enter a dark, mysterious and probably very dangerous tomb?" asked Alex.

"No, because… um… I once saw Queen Nefertari, from a distance of course, but…"

The tomb of Queen Nefertari

"Hey, Nef, wait a moment!" Alex shone the flashlight on Nef's face and grinned, "Are you blushing by any chance?"

"Leave him alone, Alex, and pass me that flashlight so we can see this room."

"Here you go… So what was so special about this queen? Come on, tell us!"

"Well, she's…. Here, take a look for yourself," added Nefer, pointing at the painting lit by Penny's flashlight, "See? She's…"

"GORGEOUS!" Alex exclaimed, enchanted by the queen's portrait.

Seeing Alex's rapt expression, Penny laughed and laughed until tears came to her eyes. "Alex is in love! Alex is in love!" she chanted, ignoring her brother's dirty looks.

DID YOU KNOW?

The name Nefertari means "the most beautiful" and the queen was undoubtedly one of the most popular and influential of ancient Egypt. Nefertari was the wife of Ramses the Grand, who dedicated countless monuments to her, including the Lesser Temple at Abu Simbel, thus immortalizing her beauty and his great love for her.

THIS MAKEUP... ISN'T JUST MADE UP!

Queen Nefertari enhanced her beauty with makeup.
This was a very widespread custom that was practiced by
both men and women, as you can see from the portraits of
ancient Egyptians, and even Nefer!

The Egyptians used makeup mainly on their eyes. They applied a dark powder called kohl to their eyelids with wooden or metal sticks to accentuate the shape of their eyes and to protect them from the desert sand and diseases.

Perfumes were also very popular and were extracted from flowers and aromatic woods, while ointments, made from animal fats, were used to protect the skin from Ra's rays. These ancient "beauty creams" were contained in little jars of all shapes, such as the one shown here.

Mirrors were an important makeup accessory, although the silver surface did not reflect a very clear image.

COLOR YOUR PHARAOH'S BREASTPLATE

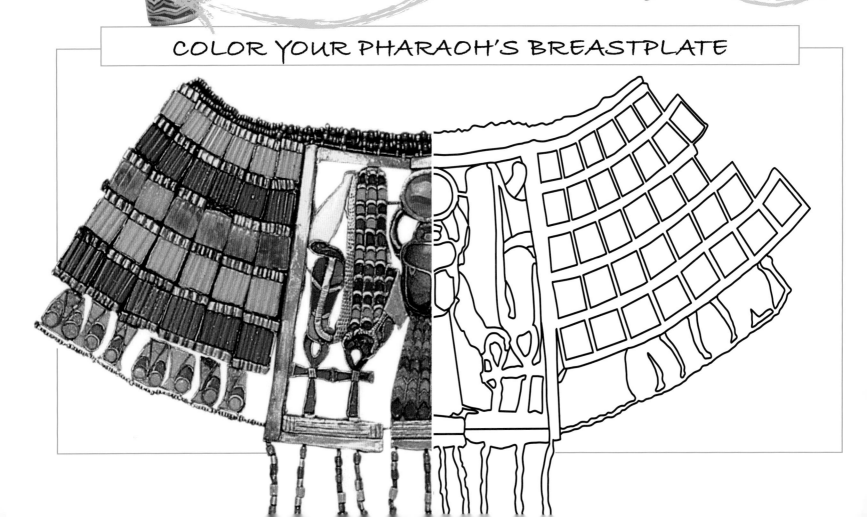

After applying their makeup, noblemen adorned themselves with necklaces and bracelets, breastplates and earrings. Some of these objects were true masterpieces, formed by inlaid gold, colored glass, beads and precious stones, which the jewelers pierced and patiently threaded onto thin strands of papyrus.

Queen Nefertari is ready to make her move on a checkerboard identical to that shown in the photo below.

CHECKING THE PHARAOH!

One of the frescoes discovered by the children during their exploration of the tomb shows Queen Nefertari playing one of the most popular ancient Egyptian games: Senet. The queen is sitting in front of a checkerboard, divided into 30 squares, on which the two opponents move their pieces. Although we do not know the rules, it is thought that Senet was a strategy game and a forerunner of chess.

THE MYSTERY OF THE SCARAB

WHERE IS THE NEXT SCARAB IS HIDDEN? FIND OUT BY READING EVERY THIRD LETTER IN A CLOCKWISE DIRECTION FROM THE ARROW.

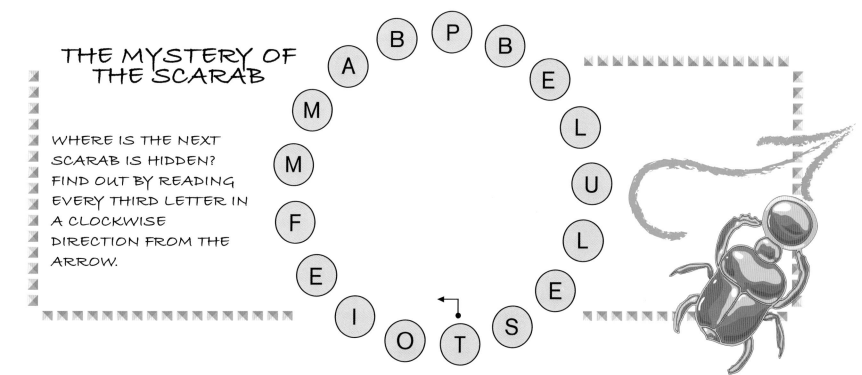

Letters around the circle (clockwise from arrow): T S E L L U L E B B P B A M M F E I O

ABU SIMBEL

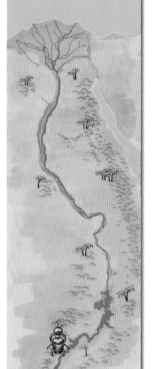

"Penny, are we there? Mew doesn't look too well. I think she's feeling airsick again."

"Just a moment, Nef, I'll check, but first I want to finish reading this chapter of Misterius' guidebook. It says that in 1966 the temple of Abu Simbel..."

"Wait a moment!" exclaimed Alex, "We've got a problem here! Epsilon's computer shows that we're about to leave Ancient Egypt!"

"That's all right," explained Nef, pleased that he knew more than the computer, "Abu Simbel is in Nubia, not Egypt."

"Nubia? What's Nubia?"

"It's a beautiful region to the south of Egypt, which is brimming with riches and inhabited by the proud and aggressive Nubians!"

"Wow! That's interesting!"

"Do you want to hear something else interesting? In 1966 the temple of Abu Simbel..."

"Hold on, Penny," Alex interrupted again, "I want to know more about the Nubians! Tell us about them, Nef!"

"OK. After centuries of battles, the pharaohs managed to conquer Nubia and built temples to celebrate their victory over the Nubians. The most important is the one of Ramses at Abu Simbel. We call it the Temple of Ramses-Meriamen, which means "beloved of Amen." The façade was entirely carved out of a rocky cliff on the west bank of the Nile."

"Yes, but in 1966 the temple of Abu Simbel –" Penny impatiently cut in.

"Stop interrupting, Penny! Carry on, Nef!"

"Look! We're here! Here's the front of the temple and the four colossal statues of Ramses, but – wait a moment – there's something wrong!"

"Of course! As I was trying to tell you, in 1966 the temple of Abu Simbel..."

"What's wrong, Nef?"

"The temple shouldn't be there! And what's that lake? That shouldn't be there! It's all changed! How can that have happened?"

"How can that have happened? I've been trying to explain it to you for half an hour!" screamed Penny, exasperated, waving Misterius' guidebook threateningly above her head.

"All right, Penny, calm down. It's not worth getting angry! Take a deep breath and explain who moved the temple. Hold on... was it the aliens?!"

"ALEX!!!"

Four colossal statues of the pharaoh Ramses were carved into the façade of the Great Temple at Abu Simbel. Each colossus is 69 feet tall, like a seven-story building!

DID YOU KNOW?

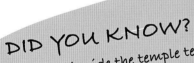

A huge relief inside the temple tells the story of Ramses' most famous battle, against the Hittites at Kadesh. Although Ramses is depicted as the absolute winner, the outcome of the battle wasn't actually decisive, and the two sides ceased hostilities by signing the first peace treaty in history.

The enormous columns of the hypostyle hall are carved to resemble Ramses II.

Careful! We're transporting Ramses' face!

WHO MOVED THE TEMPLE?

In 1960, a great danger threatened the Nubian temples: construction was about to start on a huge dam that would block the waters of the Nile and create an enormous artificial lake.

Abu Simbel and the other Nubian temples seemed condemned to disappear beneath the waters of Lake Nasser!

The news quickly traveled around the world: a solution had to be found! UNESCO, the United Nations' organization responsible for protecting the world's cultural heritage, proposed a very daring plan. Instead of moving the lake, the temples would be moved!

A salvage campaign was launched, which involved 50 countries.

The Great Temple of Abu Simbel had to be moved 215 feet higher up and 655 feet further back from its river site. In order to do this, the stone was literally cut with chainsaws and the temple divided into over 1300 individually numbered blocks. All the blocks were then transported and reassembled on the new site. The temple was thus rebuilt, maintaining the original orientation ordered by Ramses.

The blocks were then patiently reassembled.

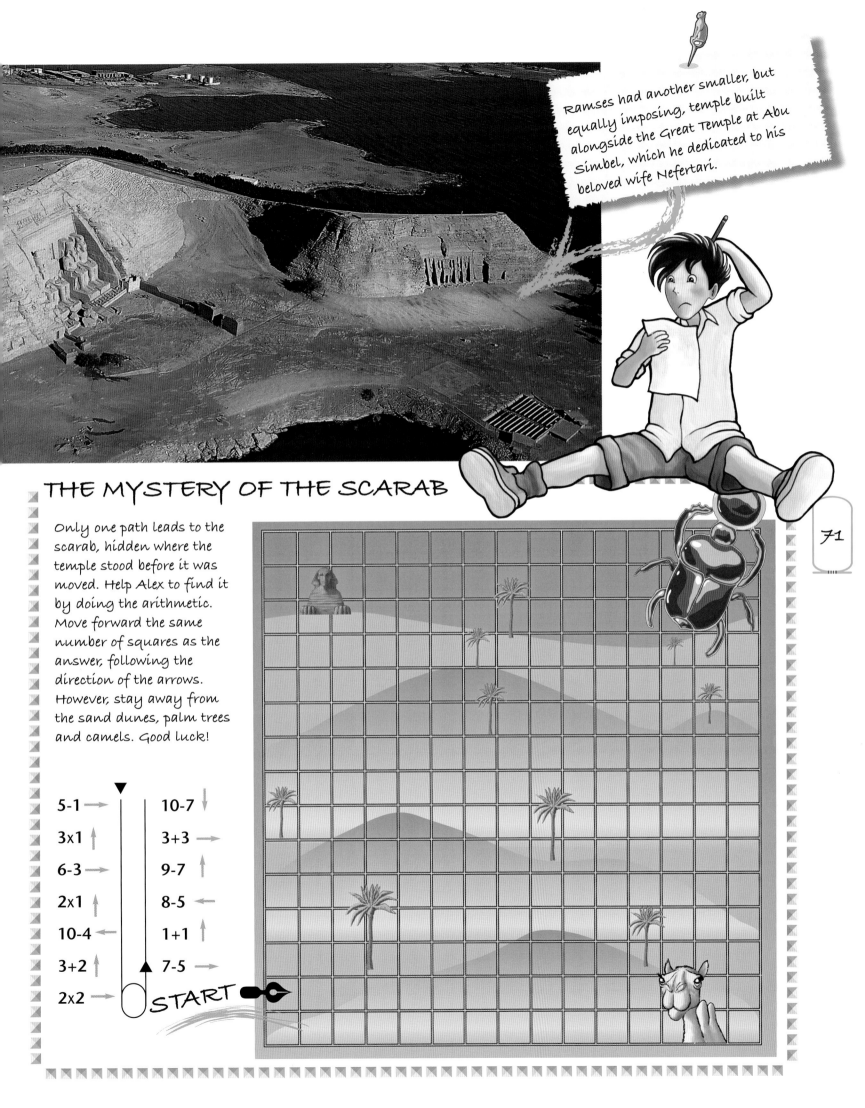

THE MYSTERY OF THE SCARAB

Only one path leads to the scarab, hidden where the temple stood before it was moved. Help Alex to find it by doing the arithmetic. Move forward the same number of squares as the answer, following the direction of the arrows. However, stay away from the sand dunes, palm trees and camels. Good luck!

5-1 →   10-7 ↓

3x1 ↑   3+3 →

6-3 →   9-7 ↑

2x1 ↑   8-5 ←

10-4 ←   1+1 ↑

3+2 ↑   7-5 →

2x2 →   START

Ramses had another smaller, but equally imposing, temple built alongside the Great Temple at Abu Simbel, which he dedicated to his beloved wife Nefertari.

Alex had flown Epsilon at top speed to return to the Sphinx as fast as possible. The children had passed through the tunnel again and had arrived in front of the magic doorway. They'd then looked around, trying to understand where to place the scarabs, and eventually Nefer had found a very clear inscription: "Lock of the Nine Keys," positioned directly above a low relief resembling a checkerboard with nine squares. The children grabbed the nine scarabs and rushed to place them on the board. They excitedly set the last one in place, but… nothing happened! Nothing at all! No door swung open and no vortex appeared! The inside of the Sphinx remained dark and silent, until Nefer and Mew realized what had happened.

"MEOWWWWWW!!"

"AAAAGGGHH!!"

The little cat and her master burst into tears.

"WE'LL NEVER GET HOME!!!!!!"

"Meowww!"

Alex and Penny were speechless with disappointment and didn't know how to console their friend. Alex gave Nefer his handkerchief, but took it back almost immediately to hide the tears that had started to come to his eyes too. Penny, on the other hand, was very thoughtful. What had happened? Had they found all the scarabs and brought them back here for nothing? Perhaps they needed to push them harder into the checkerboard, or perhaps…

"Of course! Stop crying, guys, I think I might have it!"

"Have what, Penny?" asked Alex, blowing his nose.

"Do you remember those strange signs carved into the back of the scarabs?"

"Yes… and?"

"I was wondering whether the signs could have been carved to show in which order the scarabs should be placed on the checkerboard. Perhaps the door won't open because we didn't put them in the right order! Let's turn them all over and try to join the carved signs to make a picture that makes sense!"

THE NINE SCARABS

THE NINE SCARABS MUST BE PLACED ON THE CHECKERBOARD IN EXACTLY THE RIGHT ORDER TO OPEN THE TIME PORTAL. EXAMINE THE SIGNS ON THE BACK OF THE SCARABS AND TRY TO PUT THEM IN ORDER BY DRAWING THEM ON THE CHECKERBOARD. YOU'LL KNOW YOU'VE GOT IT RIGHT WHEN YOU SEE THE PICTURE OF THE GUARDIAN OF THE PYRAMIDS APPEAR!

The stone door suddenly started to light up, becoming paler and paler until it was almost white. The children had to cover their eyes, but they still managed to see the surface of the door rippling. The stone was transformed into countless little waves of light, which gradually started to swirl together, forming a huge vortex: the time portal was open!

"Hurray!" The children started to shout with joy and leap back and forth. Mew was the first to remember that the portal would soon close, and jumped and mewed to let the children know.

"Nef, you've got to go now, before the door closes again!"

"Yes, I know… but I'm sorry to leave you guys."

"We're sorry too, Nefer, but you have to go home!"

"Hang on! I've got an idea!" The little Egyptian ran to the checkerboard with the nine scarabs, and pulled with all his might to remove one. "Listen! We can't leave all the scarabs here, can we? Otherwise anyone could use the portal and endanger both my time and yours. Here's my idea: you keep one of the scarabs and be its guardians. The portal will then be safe forever and you'll be able to open it to visit me in my time whenever you want!"

"That's a brilliant idea, Nefer!" Alex exclaimed.

"We'll be the guardians of the portal that the high priest was seeking!" added Penny.

"See you soon then!" said Nefer, picking up Mew and tossing the scarab to Alex before jumping into the vortex of light!

"See you soon, Nefer!"

SOLUTIONS

PAGE 18

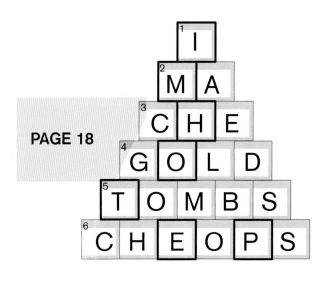

PAGE 23

PAGE 20

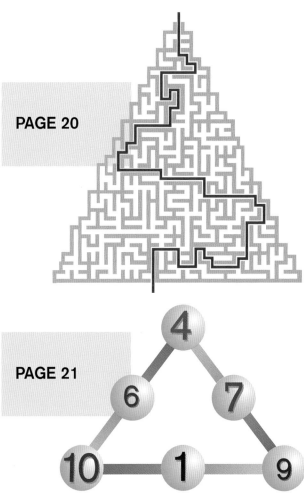

PAGE 24

HARVEST

FLOOD

SOWING

AKHET

PERET

SHEMU

PAGE 21

PAGE 25

Abu carries the goose across the river first of all, then returns to fetch the dog and leaves it on the opposite bank, taking the goose back with him. He then crosses the river again with the grain, before returning one last time to fetch the goose. He thus never leaves the dog alone with the goose, or the goose alone with the grain!

PAGE 21

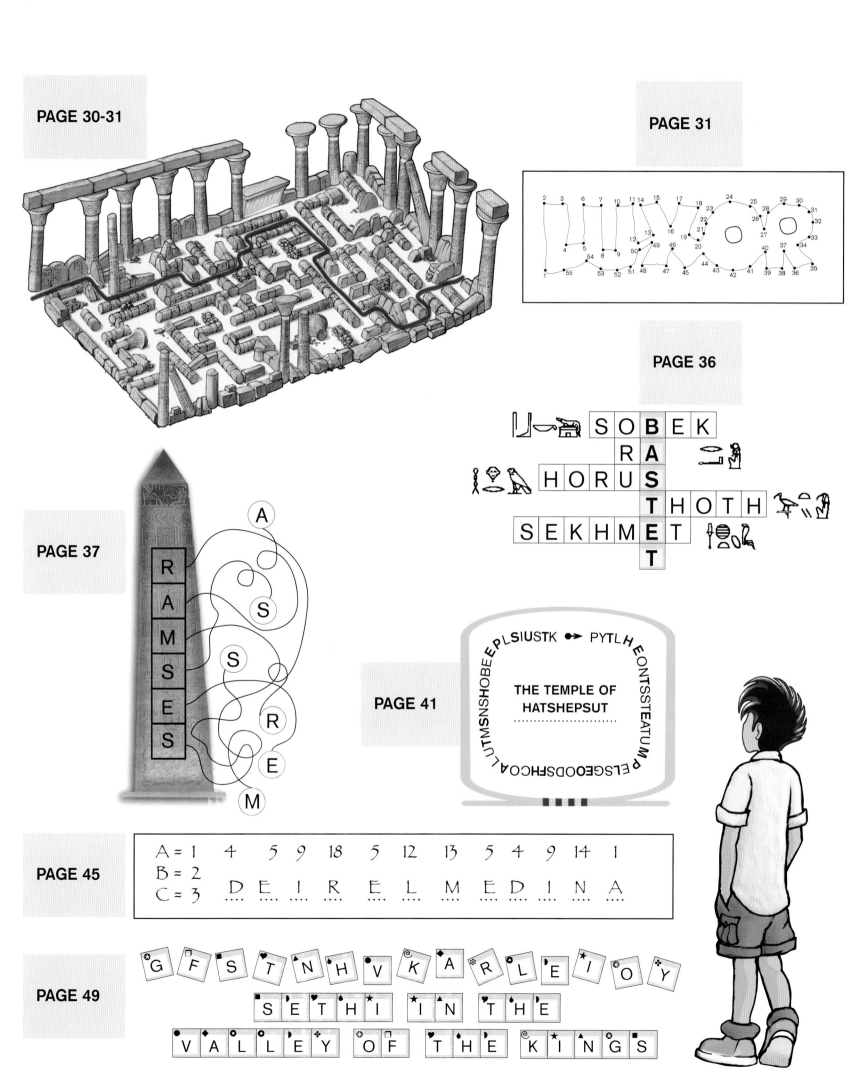

PAGE 30-31

PAGE 31

PAGE 36

SOBEK
R A
HORUS
T H O T H
SEKHMET

PAGE 37

A
R
A
M S
S
E S
S R
E
M

PAGE 41

THE TEMPLE OF HATSHEPSUT
....

PAGE 45

A ≈ 1
B ≈ 2
C ≈ 3

4   5   9   18   5   12   13   5   4   9   14   1
D   E   I   R   E   L   M   E   D   I   N   A

PAGE 49

G F S T N H V K A R L E I O Y
S E T H I   I N   T H E
V A L L E Y   O F   T H E   K I N G S

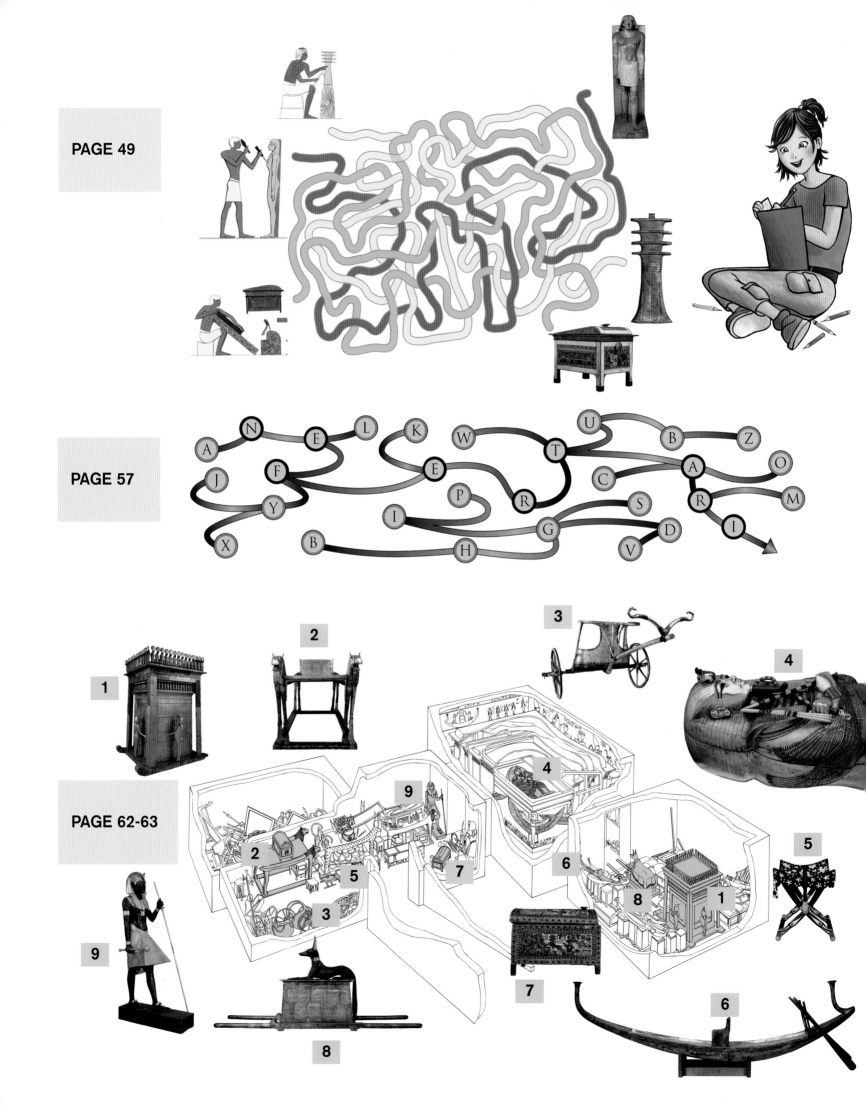

PAGE 49

PAGE 57

PAGE 62-63

PAGE 67

TEMPLE OF ABU SIMBEL

PAGE 71

79

5-1 →	**4**	10-7 ↓	**3**
3x1 ↑	**3**	3+3 →	**6**
6-3 →	**3**	9-7 ↑	**2**
2x1 ↑	**2**	8-5 ←	**3**
10-4 ←	**6**	1+1 ↑	**2**
3+2 ↑	**5**	7-5 →	**2**
2x2 →	**4**		

PAGE 73

www.alexepenny.it

EDITORIAL COORDINATION
GIADA FRANCIA

TEXTS
GIADA FRANCIA

GRAPHIC DESIGNER
PATRIZIA BALOCCO LOVISETTI

ARTWORK
ANGELO COLOMBO

PHOTO CREDITS

All photographs are by Araldo De Luca/Archivio White Star except the following:

Archivio White Star: pages 24-25, 26-27, 37 bottom, 47, 49 left, 52 top, 53 bottom, 62-63, 68

Antonio Attini/Archivio White Star: pages 2 (fourth photo), 29

Marcello Bertinetti/Archivio White Star: pages 2 (first and third photo), 3 (third photo), 8 center, 10 left and right, 16-17, 18 left, 19, 22-23, 27, 28-29, 32, 38-39, 42, 43, 45, 46-47, 50, 68-69, 70-71

The British Museum: pages 41 right, 48 top right, 48 bottom right

Giovanni Dagli Orti/Art Archive: page 56 top

Farabola: pages 70 top, center and bottom

Elisabetta Ferrero/Archivio White Star: pages 18 right, 20-21, 56-57, 60-61

Griffith Institute, Ashmolean Museum Oxford: pages 60, 61

Alfio Garozzo/Archivio White Star: pages 37 center, 38 right

Les frères Chuzeville/Photo RMN: page 53 left

Alberto Siliotti/Geodia: page 41 left, 54

Giulio Veggi/Archivio White Star: pages 2 (second photo), 3 (first photo), 32-33, 38 left

© 2006 White Star S.p.A.
Via Candido Sassone, 22/24
13100 Vercelli, Italy
www.whitestar.it

Translation: Sarah Ponting
Editing: Sara Newberry

ISBN-10: 88-544-0159-5
ISBN-13: 978-88-544-0159-4

Reprint:
1 2 3 4 5 6   10 09 08 07 06

Printed in India
Color separation by: Fotomec, Turin, Italy